TRAVEL LIGHTLY
Unpacking Burdensome Baggage

by

Dr. Craig L. Oliver, Sr.

TABLE OF CONTENTS

DEDICATION

I dedicate this book, first and foremost, to my lovely wife, Chi'Ira and my three amazing children—my son, Craig Jr. and my daughters, Corrie Kené and Charlee Reign. Without your constant love and support, I could never have completed this work. Each of you makes my joy complete.

To my mom and dad,
    Thank you for your constant wisdom, love and support.

To the Oliver family,
    We've been through so much as all families have, but love and the grace of God has seen us through it—thank you.

To the entire Elizabeth Baptist Church family in Atlanta, Smyrna, Douglasville, Fairburn and Conyers,
    I hope this book blesses you as much as you have blessed me to be your pastor.

ACKNOWLEDGEMENTS

I want to thank Almighty God and his Son, our Lord Jesus Christ, without whom there would be no reason to write, to preach or to do anything.

I want to acknowledge:

My mentor, Pastor J.E. Hightower—your years of wisdom and guidance have helped me in innumerable ways.

My host of friends, resisting the urge to name each of you — your undying friendship is one of my most beloved treasures. I can always count on each of you for a laugh no matter what I'm going through.

The Collaborative Preaching Team and the wonderful Staff and Leadership Team of Elizabeth Baptist Church —each of you makes my burden lighter in so many ways.

A special shout out to staff members Nicole Lester and Lisa Childers who worked especially hard getting this book together— taking meticulous notes and organizing all the details to bring this dream to fruition. Great job. Thank you.

To every member of Elizabeth Baptist Church who work hard in the fields for the glory of the Lord. Thank you for honoring me beyond words in serving as your pastor.

Finally, to each of you readers—thank you. I pray that you are freed of your burdens and able to Travel Lightly through the rest of your journey.

~Craig L. Oliver Sr.

FOREWORD BY DR. SAM CHAND

Have you ever seen a US Marine pulling a suitcase through the airport? People on a mission prepare for their travel, not with more but with less. Less is more.

My friend Dr. Craig L. Oliver admonishes us to travel lightly. One would think that as life happens and we mature that we would learn this lesson on our own. That is not the case.

The question is rarely *what* is slowing you down or holding you back. It is always *who* is impeding your progress.

I'm on about two hundred flights a year and always have carry-on luggage. However, when I get to my destination, people often give me gifts that either don't fit in my suitcase or make it too heavy for me to hoist into the overhead space in the airplane. Because I want to travel lightly, I often ask my hosts to ship those gifts to my home. This teaches me a few things about light travel when it comes to my internal being:

- Just because someone offers me more to pack doesn't mean I have to find a place for it and pack it.
- Some of my *burdensome baggage* is real, and this book helps me to understand and unpack it.
- Most of my *burdensome baggage* is perceived, third-hand, or cumulative imaginations; and these are the most difficult to unpack.

Don't feel bad if your suitcase is burgeoning and the zipper is about to bust. Life is that way. We accumulate burdensome baggage and don't have an intentional strategy to continuously unpack it.

Dr. Oliver is right when he admonishes us to travel lightly. That's what Jesus did when sending out His ambassadors in Luke 10:4: *"Travel light. Comb and toothbrush and no extra luggage"* (MSG, italics added).

Samuel R. Chand

Dr. Sam Chand
Leadership Architect and Change Strategist at Samuel R. Chand Consulting; Dream Releaser Consulting; Dream Releaser Publishing, Author of *Leadership Pain*

FOREWORD BY DR. KENNETH C. ULMER

My first trip to South Africa was in April 1990, two months after Dr. Nelson Mandela was released from Robben Island after twenty-seven years of incarceration for being an advocate and activist for freedom for millions of black South Africans. Among my most prized possessions is a picture taken with him in the backyard of the house where he was raised. My life was forever changed, and I have been there every year since then.

One of the honors and joys of my travels to South Africa is to experience and be blessed by the cultural spirit of hospitality and honor they shower upon visitors. After several visits, I was received more as one returning home than a visitor, and I was often overwhelmed by the generosity of my various hosts. I have received everything from antelope skins to bows and arrows to numerous statues and statuettes—even a gorgeous blanket presented by a loving pastor in which he wrapped my wife and me as an expression of love, comfort for my journey, and a reminder of our time together. However, as joyous as these regular excursions have been, one of them accounts for the most frustrating journey of my life.

I had received several gifts from my hosts, and I had purchased other trinkets and souvenirs in addition to my regular traveling garb. I pack rather heavily since I usually am scheduled to speak several times and am required to make several wardrobe changes, sometimes several in a day.

This time I was on my way home, and as I pushed the heavy-laden cart to the ticket agent at the Oliver Tambo International Airport, she raised her eyebrows as I struggled to put several pieces of my luggage on the scale. She looked at me and scowled. Then she spoke in the beautiful South African dialect: "Sir, you have too much baggage." I quickly snapped at her, "I can pay for it!" She looked at the scales, counted the bags, and started calculating. She looked in a book on the counter and calculated some more. Finally she said, "Sir, it's going to cost you a lot of money to pay for the extra bag and the extra weight. You have too much weight and too many bags."

I thought I would redistribute the weight of the already bulging suitcases, so I stepped out of line and desperately tried to swap items from one fat piece to a slightly less-fat piece. With beads of sweat starting to trickle down my face, I strained to smile as I approached the counter again, assured that I had settled the problem.

This time she didn't even put the bags on the scale. She said, "Sir we still have a problem." I quickly informed her of my tedious task of redistributing the weight of the bags. She looked at me, by now seemingly as frustrated as I was, and said, "Sir, you don't understand. You have two problems. First of all, your bags are too heavy. You have too much weight. But the biggest problem is, you have too many bags! You are only allowed two bags. You have three!"

I began to argue that I had the same number of bags that I brought when I entered the country almost two weeks before. She went on to explain that there had been some kind of rule change and travelers were only allowed two bags. I argued that they should have told me that when I left Los Angeles. She said they should have, but somebody must have let me slide and allowed me on the plane. Again she sternly told me that I had too much weight and too many bags and I could not board the plane. She said, "Sir, you have to get rid of one of the bags and lose some of the weight."

By now my biggest struggle was to do my best to remain "spiritual" and not let my thoughts come out in the words that were on my tongue! My mind flashed to the morning headlines, "American Preacher Jailed for Cussing Ticket Agent!" Lord, have mercy!

My assistant stepped in and spoke up. He told me he only had one bag that wasn't full. He said we could put one of my bags on his ticket and we could rearrange the weight between our four bags.

It took another half hour to accomplish this gargantuan task. I boarded the plane with a great lesson. It costs too much to travel with heavy bags; it costs too much to travel with too many bags.

God has sovereignly navigated your journey to this powerful work. You hold in your hands a tool with advice, warnings, and instructions on the spiritual ability and advantage of traveling light. You will learn the dangers of too much baggage. You will be blessed by the various descriptions of the kinds of baggage we accumulate in life's journey. Most of all, you will learn the available deliverance you can have and the great Deliverer who will share your load and lighten your load.

Grace be upon you as you learn the spiritual art of *Travel Lightly*.

Kenneth C. Ulmer, DMin, PhD
Senior Pastor, Faithful Central Bible Church
Los Angeles, CA

PRAISE FOR *Travel Lightly*

"If you were to meet my friend Dr. Craig Oliver Sr., you would quickly notice his love for his Lord, his commitment to the sound Biblical exegesis and his passion to articulate the profound truths of scripture into the lives of people. Which is exactly what you will discover in his new book, "Travel Lightly." If you struggle with being "weary and heavy-laden," then I have great news for you. In the pages of this book you will find clarity as to what is weighing you down and why. You will also discover practical principles you can utilize to "off-load" all the excess baggage you were never meant to carry and walk in the freedom Christ died to give us. Thanks Craig for your transparency and wisdom. Well done, my friend!"

Dr. Bruce Hebel
President, ReGenerating Life Ministries,
coauthor of *Forgiving Forward*

For years I have been blessed by the preaching and ministry of Dr. Craig Oliver, Sr. He preaches with profound integrity to the biblical text and homiletical skill that impacts listeners. Without a doubt, he is a great expositor of the gospel, and his proficiency in preaching has contributed greatly to this work. Dr. Oliver has taken the skill and precision he has used in the pulpit for years and has used it to deliver an impactful, practical, and theologically strong work around the emotions that hold back individuals. Readers of this work will undoubtedly receive relevant writing to handle the variety of emotions that can prevent them from living up to their God-given potential.

Dr. James Merrit
Senior Pastor, Cross Pointe Church
Former President, Southern Baptist Convention

Dr. Craig Oliver has written a book that puts its finger on the places where people hurt. His book is not a recipe of "how-to-do" fixes, but rather he has given us words for life to salve those hurts when life happens. It is not a matter of if these hurts will come, but when will they come. Everyone will experience these troubles at one time or another. Those in these seasons of life, Dr. Oliver encourages to choose to love the Lord with all their hearts and learn to live in God's presence. Dr. Oliver has given us a beautiful book of encouragement that will restore one's joy for living.

Dr. David L. Mapes
Associate Professor of Theology,
Luther Rice Seminary

"Dr. Craig Oliver is achieving two grand objectives in his book Traveling Light. The first is to challenge the reader and encourage the adherer to consider how much luggage it really takes to make a successful journey through life. Once that question is answered, the next step is to make adjustments. The lighter you pack, the easier it is to travel. Besides, you want to leave space in life's luggage to pick up some new essentials along the way.

The second objective Dr. Oliver makes is to imitate the travel habits of Jesus. Once, Jesus sent His disciples on a fact-finding mission to travel in pairs to every town and place. He told them not to take too much money, not to take extra sandals, not to move from house to house, and to eat what was given to them. Jesus tells us to pack peace and leave it as a gift in the homes of the confused. Don't forget to pack healing for all those people you meet who are sick—sick of being addicted to the temporal and sick of trying to satisfy the spiritual with the material. Then leave room in your backpack to take the homeless message of the kingdom of God.

Travel light so you can travel right; travel light, and you'll live in the marvelous light."

Dr. Ralph Douglas West
Pastor and Founder of The Church Without Walls
(Brookhollow Baptist Church), Houston, TX

"Pastor Craig Oliver's sermons are outstanding examples of "standing between two worlds"—the world of the text and the world of the congregation. Each chapter is biblically grounded and personally and culturally relevant. What could be more relevant than shedding the light of God's Word on the "baggage" we carry around? Although the chapters are written communication, they carry the echo of spoken discourse from the original sermons. I can hear Dr. Oliver's voice in these pages. Good preaching has become good reading."

Dr. Jeffrey Arthurs
Professor of Preaching and Communication;
Chair, Division of Practical Theology
Gordon Conwell Theological Seminary

TRAVEL LIGHTLY

INTRODUCTION
Unpacking Burdensome Baggage

"Wherefore seeing we also are compassed about with so great a cloud of witnesses, let us lay aside every weight, and the sin which doth so easily beset us, and let us run with patience the race that is set before us."
(Hebrews 12:1)

You may love it, but I admit that I hate packing luggage. I dread—no, I *disdain*—with every fiber of my body, the entire process of packing luggage. I consider it one of the unnecessary evils of life. Anticipating the clothes I'll need and having to arrange them in some suitcase so I can maximize the space just irritates me.

I think packing bothers me because I travel so much. If I only traveled once or twice a year, I might not find it so frustrating; but I often travel two to three times per *week*. Packing and unpacking takes significant time away from my busy schedule. That is why, some time ago, I developed a habit that has served me well as I travel. It's based on a simple philosophy I like to call "travel lightly." This little philosophy has helped me in more ways than I can describe.

I first developed this philosophy when the airlines decided to charge an extra twenty-five dollars for each bag. Although I am a frequent flyer and don't have to worry about those fees myself, I pay for the bags of those who travel with me, which created a tremendous economic incentive for this new philosophy.

Years ago, my travel itinerary began to increase as I was invited to speak in different places around the country. As a result I packed using the philosophy, "Better safe than sorry." That meant I traveled with a back-up plan that accounted for every possible contingency. I preferred to have it and not need it rather than to need it and not have it. What if I spilled ketchup on my shirt? scuffed my shoes? bent over and split the seat of my pants? What if I had a wardrobe malfunction? I had to be prepared.

On top of that, I was speaking on different platforms. I felt I had to make a good impression on people by dressing my best. If I were going away for a multi-day event, I packed several suits, ties, and shoes. I'd struggle through the airports with so many bags that, if it weren't for the suit I was wearing, people could have mistaken me for a skycap.

Since the airlines started charging—and now that I'm older and wiser—I realize there are a few tricks that make it easier to travel lightly. Nowadays, I pack one suit and a few ties. When I finish speaking, I send my suit to be dry-cleaned and wear it again the next day. All I've got to do is switch up the tie, and people think I have on a brand-new suit—no one can tell the difference. I no longer care if the shoes match the ties; one pair of black or brown shoes will do fine. If I spill something on a shirt, I'll have it cleaned or retrieve one of the additional ones packed. I rarely spill anything anyway. It was something I worried about that wasn't actually a problem for me. Lots of things in life, in fact, can be like that—things that aren't actually a problem for us.

Unfortunately, I'm the only person in my family who understands and appreciates this new philosophy. My travel partner and wife, Cleo, has not embraced my philosophy yet. We often have "intense verbal exchanges" (code for *arguments*) over the fact that she still finds it necessary to pack both house and home on every trip.

I wouldn't mind so much except that, as the man of the house, I'm the one who ends up lugging her excess baggage through the airport, which as you can imagine, kind of defeats the purpose of the philoso-

> WE HAVE THE TENDENCY TO CARRY MORE THAN WHAT WE NEED TO CARRY ON THE JOURNEY OF LIFE. NO WONDER MANY OF US STRUGGLE.

phy. Perhaps you can understand why I get so vexed about having to carry a lot of excess baggage and why I choose to travel lightly.

I have learned how to travel lightly when I fly, but I don't believe my philosophy only applies to journeys through airports. As we go through life, it would benefit us to learn how to travel lightly in other ways. Too many people go through life carrying burdensome baggage—baggage that weighs down the soul and the human spirit. We have the tendency to carry more than what we need to carry on the journey of life. No wonder many of us struggle with hypertension, stress, and other physical ailments. Could it be we carry too much baggage?

Of course, I'm not talking about actual baggage but the intangible, invisible baggage we all carry internally in our minds and in our hearts:

- The Draining Duffle Bag of Depression, Doubt, and Defeatism
- The Agonizing Attaché Case of Anxiety
- The Heavy Handbag of Hopelessness
- The Grievous Garment Bag of Guilt
- The Loathsome Luggage of Low Self-Esteem
- The Frightening Flip Bag of Fear
- The Bulging Backpack of Bitterness
- The Ugly Utility Bag of Unforgiveness

We all have baggage. I have it, you have it—all of us have some type of baggage that we carry around with us everywhere we go.

My purpose in this book is to encourage you to make the decision to lay aside some of the baggage you've carried for so long. You do not need to remain burdened down. You don't have to let it steal your joy, your peace, or your faith. You can stop now. Today!

It is up to you, however, to realize that there is some baggage you must let go. God is not going to take it away from you. You must resolve that you want to release the baggage. I believe that's what the author of Hebrews wrote about in the central passage of Scripture we'll use to help us deal with our burdensome baggage.

Hebrews 12:1-3 gives us the master plan for getting rid of burdensome baggage. The writer of Hebrews dealt with an audience of converted Jewish believers who, faced with increasing opposition to and persecution for their new faith, were tempted to return to their previous practice of Judaism. These new believers struggled with alienation and the loss of ties to loved ones who considered them to have betrayed the Jewish faith. They dealt with persecution by Jewish leaders. They dealt with being social outcasts. Moreover, they dealt with the temptation to return to Judaism. Returning to their former faith would fix so many of these believers' problems: relieving their persecution, reuniting them with their families, and restoring their standing in society. The author of Hebrews came to them to exhort, challenge, and encourage them to stay with Christ because they had a better covenant with Him than what they had in Judaism.

The author wants to keep these Hebrew believers from giving in to the temptation to go back to what they had before. He begins by showing them how much better faith in Christ is than the promises of the Torah, which their ancestors relied on. He describes Christ as the fulfillment of God's promises in the Scriptures. He recounts dozens of stories from the Scriptures and shows how they were a mere foreshadowing of the work of Christ on the cross.

The author's argument starts in Chapter 11, where he masterfully commences with the creation of the universe and explains how all that we understand about God is by and through faith. He then works his way from Adam through Abraham, Moses and the prophets, explaining how these heroes endured all they suffered throughout history because of their faith in a mere promise of salvation, that they never received in their lifetimes, but which was fulfilled in Jesus Christ's death, burial, and resurrection.

The writer of Hebrews exhorts and cheers on these believers to keep running in faith. He admonishes them by declaring, "Wherefore seeing we also are compassed about with so great a cloud of witnesses, let us lay aside every weight, and the sin which doth so easily beset us, and let us run with patience the race that is set before us" (Hebrews 12:1).

As children of God, we all have a race to run. The only way we can really run that race is if we follow the three injunctions, or commands, found in this verse. The first injunction we must follow is to "lay aside" some stuff. Lay aside your weights, the sin that easily entangles you so that you can run with endurance. The author uses the metaphor of the Greek Olympic Games to describe this race that each believer must run. The weight that the Hebrew believers were to "lay aside" in their context constitutes the trappings and traditions of Judaism coupled with the "besetting sin" of faithlessness, which were hindrances in their walk with God.

We in the Christian race as well have weights that we must "lay aside." I submit to you that this stuff, namely "weights," we must lay aside in order to run the race can also be described as our baggage. That word *weight* in the original Greek language of the New Testament is *ogkos*, meaning "that which is bulky, a mass, burden, or hindrance." It is the cumulative stuff that weighs us down and encumbers us with cares. It is that which holds you down or holds you back. The author of Hebrews says you must lay aside not just *some* stuff but *every* weight that hinders your progress.

There are three reasons that these *ogkos*, or weights, must be laid aside. The first reason is holding on to baggage will impede your progress. Most people can lift five pounds. Most of us would agree that five pounds is relatively light. Imagine, however, if you had to run a sprint or a marathon wearing five-pound ankle weights. If you're not a runner, imagine walking and living for years with the same ankle weights attached to you everywhere you go. Although the weight is relatively insignificant, it would still impede your progress and become excessively burdensome. You cannot run or walk swiftly with endurance or with a high degree of stamina when you are weighed down.

The same is true in life. If you go through life carrying "baggage," you will not progress the way you want because of the extra weight. In fact, ask yourself whether there were goals you wanted to accomplish this year that you failed to accomplish because of some baggage you were holding onto from last year. Had you rid yourself of that baggage, you may have met your goals; but holding onto baggage and refusing or being unable to let it go hindered you. Holding on to baggage will impede your progress.

The second reason you must let go of baggage is that it impacts your partnerships. There is a three-fold partnership impact of holding on to baggage. First, it will impact your partnership with the Omnipotent. David, in Psalm 51, carried the baggage of guilt, shame, and condemnation and found he needed to pray, "Restore unto me the joy of thy salvation" (verse 12) because his partnership with the Omnipotent was not what it used to be. David's soul was miserable, and his disposition was melancholy at best.

When we walk around with unconfessed sin, guilt, shame, or a sense of condemnation, it directly impacts our fellowship with God. It is hard to walk in fellowship with God while carrying baggage. For David, it robbed him of the joy of his salvation.

Second, baggage also impacts our partnership with ourselves. Jesus says we are to love the Lord with all of our hearts, with all of our minds, and all of our souls and that we are to love our neighbors *as ourselves*. Dr. Kenneth Boa, in his book, *Conformed to His Image: Biblical and Practical Approaches to Spiritual Formation*, put it this way: "We are to love the Lord our God *completely*—with all of our mind, all of our soul and all of our hearts, but then we are to love ourselves *correctly* so that we can love others *compassionately*."[1]

You will never be able to love others as you ought if you don't love yourself correctly. Many of us have a warped sense of love for ourselves. We don't love ourselves, and so we aren't able to truly love others as we ought. If we don't love ourselves, we don't embrace ourselves, and we don't care for ourselves. Furthermore, if we can't care for ourselves, we have a hard time loving others.

In addition to impacting our partnership with God and ourselves, walking around with baggage also impacts our partnership and connection with others. Have you ever had a difficult time maintaining a wholesome, healthy relationship? Do you find that people are always in and out of your life? Have you ever wondered why it seems as if no one wants to hang out with you, wants to deal with you, or wants to be with you? It could possibly be because you carry too much burdensome baggage.

Lugging around too much baggage can make you a negative and bitter person. Perhaps you know people who only have negative things to say. You ask them, "How was your day?" They answer, "Well, it could be better." Nothing is ever good enough. Nothing positive ever flows form their lips. Their conversations are negative, and they wonder why no one wants to hang out with them.

You dig a little deeper and discover that this person is still angry with her ex-husband who left her twenty years ago, or he's still ticked off at the driver who cut him off on the highway last week. That's how holding onto baggage works; it adversely affects our partnerships with other people. Please don't believe the hype. People aren't really excited to attend the pity parties we often unintentionally host. Personally, I've yet to attend a pity party where refreshments are served. So holding on to baggage impedes our progression (places our lives in neutral or reverse) and impacts our partnerships (adversely affects our social/spiritual interactions).

Third, we must let go of baggage because it serves as an impasse to our peace. God desires us to experience His peace. When you walk around burdened, you can never experience His peace that surpasses all understanding. Your sense of spiritual serenity, security, and stability is shaken. A deep sense of contentment in Christ is thwarted because you have too much baggage cluttering up your soul—the seat of your inner life.

How do you deal with this excessive and expensive baggage?

I will address the specifics types of baggage throughout this book, but here are three quick actions that can help you reduce all types of baggage.

The first is *acknowledgement*. Hebrews 12:1 says, "Let us lay aside every weight." You can't lay aside the baggage in your life if you don't acknowledge that it exists. Bottom line—if you don't want to confess it and confront it, you can't correct it.

Consider how many times we go through life playing baggage patrol. We happily point out the baggage in everyone else's life but woefully neglect to identify the baggage in our own lives. If you're not like that, perhaps you know some professional baggage inspectors—spiritual TSA agents. They want to open your baggage and look at what's in your life but not deal with their own bags. If you're going to deal with your baggage and get rid of the stuff that's weighing you down, you must first acknowledge that you have baggage. In fact, say it out loud now: "I have baggage." It's not your neighbor, your spouse, your siblings, or your children. No, it's you. You have baggage.

You carry historic stuff that has wrecked your life in the past and that is still messing you up now: A bitter spirit. A sense of anxiety. A spirit of unforgiveness. A sense of guilt. A sense of shame. You've got a whole lot of baggage to deal with. If you don't deal with it, *it* will continue to deal with *you*. And if you're going to deal with your baggage, the first thing you must do is acknowledge it exists. Say it again: "I have baggage!"

Second, *abandonment* helps you deal with your baggage. "Let us lay aside," means abandon it. Get rid of it. God does not want you to walk around with baggage. He wants you to have life and have it more abundantly. You cannot enjoy the abundant life God has for you when you walk around with baggage. He says, "I've come to set you free. And whom the Son sets free is free indeed" (John 8:36).

The freedom Jesus Christ offers comes in a plethora of refreshing ways. He wants to free you from guilt, shame, and bitterness. He wants to free you from that sense of hopelessness, from depression, and from having a victim mentality. He wants to free you from defeatism, from anger, from fear; but to get free, you must not only acknowledge your baggage, you must also be determined that, through the power of Christ, you are going to abandon it. You must resolve that you are no longer going to live in bondage to your baggage.

You may be asking, "How can I abandon it?" That's a good question, because if you're trying to do it on your own, you're not likely to succeed. But thank God that Paul wrote in Philippians 4:13, "I can do all things through Christ, who strengthens me." Even when you are weak, even when you feel helpless, even when you can't do it, you can do all things through Christ who lives in you in the person of the Holy Spirit.

It is only through faith in the enabling power of Jesus Christ that we are liberated from baggage. In regards to living a fruitful life, Jesus declared to His disciples, "I am the vine; you are the branches. If you remain in me and I in you, you will bear much fruit; apart from me you can do nothing (John 15:5, NIV). This key biblical principle holds true not only as it relates to living a fruitful life, but also as it relates to a freed life. Without Jesus Christ, you can do nothing.

How does it work? There's a difference between "I can" and "I will." "I can" is *potentiality*. "I will" is *performance*. Let me explain it this way: I can lose weight (potentiality). However, the problem with potentiality is that it is no good if there's no performance to back it up. If I had no discipline yesterday or the day before, it doesn't matter how much I talk about what I *can* do. I have to move from *can* to *will*—from talk to action.

Another way to express this idea is to juxtapose divine sovereignty and human responsibility. When Jesus raised Lazarus from the dead, He used His divine sovereignty to do it, which was manifested through His supernatural power to raise the dead. However, before He did, He told the disciples to roll away the stone. There was action taken by the disciples as well—that is human responsibility. When Jesus fed the five thousand, a little boy offered his food—human responsibility. Jesus used His divine sovereignty to multiply the lad's lunch. In Philippians 2:13, Paul says that God wills in us to do what we, in ourselves, cannot do. So there must be an acknowledgement of your baggage along with a resolute attitude of abandonment.

Third, there must be *advancement*. Notice the interjections in Hebrews 12:1-2. We are told to "look ahead." Look unto Jesus. Why? What did Jesus do? He ran His race; He advanced continuously until He completed the race. In Chapter 11, the writer of Hebrews walks us through the "Hall of Faith" with all of the heroic predecessors of faith from the Old Testament. However, in Chapter 12, he tells us that Jesus is the Author and Finisher of our faith.

As Author, Jesus is the Pioneer. As Finisher, He is the perfector. He is our example and the true hero of the faith because, just as you have a race to run, our Lord Jesus Christ also had a race to run. He started His race when, after forty-two generations, He was born in Bethlehem. He ran His race to the Temple where He began to teach at the age of twelve, baffling the minds of the religious leaders. He kept running His race by giving sight to the blind, enabling the lame to walk, and giving power to the weak. He ran His race to Gethsemane where He took the bitter cup—where Peter, James, and John went to sleep on Him. He ran His race all the way to Golgotha, to Calvary, where He suffered, bled, and died—and where the Book of Hebrews says He "endured the cross and despised the shame."

What made Him run the race? Verse 2 says that Jesus sought joy at the finish line. He kept on running until three days later . . . you know what happened . . . He rose from the grave. Hebrews says He is still doing something right now. He sits, at this very moment, at the right hand of the Father making intercession for us. For when we are weak, we have the Author and the Finisher of our faith praying for us. When you feel like throwing in the towel, when you feel like hanging your head, when you feel like giving up, Jesus is praying for you. You have Jesus helping you with your bags. You are not alone. You have all the power you need to help you advance to the finish line. We are to advance forward, looking to Jesus for inspiration, as we are the beneficiaries of His intercession that strengthens us on our journey.

Remember how I hate carrying baggage? On one particular trip, we left the house, and Cleo, as usual, packed up all her luggage. I, as usual, was upset. Cleo had our daughter Charlee in one hand.

Our daughter Corrie held her bag in her hand. Our son, C. J., carried his bag. My mother-in-law had her bags and coat in her hands. But, as the only man on the trip, I knew that Southern hospitality and etiquette required that I had to, at the very least, carry the luggage.

However, something different happened this time. When we arrived at Hartsfield-Jackson International Airport, a man came to the car from behind the ticket counter and took our luggage, placed it on a cart, checked us in, and gave us our tickets and a claim check for our bags. He placed our luggage on a belt, where it promptly disappeared. To my relief and surprise, I didn't have to carry any of the bags.

Aboard the plane, I enjoyed the flight until we were about to land. At that point, I thought about all those bags I'd have to carry once we picked them up at baggage claim, but another strange thing happened. When we got off the plane in Chicago's Midway Airport and arrived at the baggage carousel, another man came up to me and asked if he could help me with my bags. I told him, "Sure," with a sigh of relief.

"All you have to do is point out which bags are yours," he said.

I pointed and said, "That one. That one. That one. That one. That one. That one and that one."

He took each one, put them on another cart, walked us outside,

WE ALL HAVE ONE WHO IS CAPABLE AND COMPETENT AND POWERFUL TO HELP US WITH OUR BAGGAGE. HIS NAME IS JESUS, AND HE IS MORE THAN ABLE AND WILLING TO HELP YOU WITH YOUR BAGGAGE.

and hailed a cab. I got upset again thinking about having to move each of the bags from the cart to the cab, but the cab driver came from the other side of the cab, took the bags off the cart, and put them in the cab. On the way to the hotel, I again got a little bothered thinking of how I'd have to haul all those bags up to the rooms; but at the hotel, a man with a white cap came out and asked, "Sir, may I help you with your bags?"

I said, "You sure can."

He took the bags, gave me a ticket, and said, "As soon as you are checked in, we will bring the bags up to your room."

Needless to say, I was overjoyed.

We all have One who is capable and competent and powerful to help us with our baggage. His name is Jesus, and He is more than able and willing to help you with your baggage. He can lift your heavy burdens and help you travel lightly. Not to domesticate His divinity, but Jesus desires to help us with our baggage, regardless of its size or what it's stuffed with.

Throughout this book, we will take a look at different types of baggage and the effects of that baggage on your life. In each chapter, we'll explore the effects of the spiritual, mental, physical, and emotional baggage that weigh you down and demonstrate what you can do to unload them from your life.

My prayer for you, as you read this book, is that you will acknowledge your baggage, choose to abandon it, and advance in your faith toward a closer, baggage-free, relationship with Jesus Christ. It's time to break free from the weights that so easily hinder you by dropping the excess baggage and determining to travel lightly.

Join me on the journey.

CHAPTER ONE
The Draining Duffle Bag of Depression, Doubt, and Defeatism

"Thou holdest mine eyes waking:
I am so troubled that I cannot speak."
(Psalm 77:4)

The first bag I'll address is one of the most serious. As I write this, Academy Award-winning actor and comedian Robin Williams recently committed suicide. Later investigations revealed that the highly successful actor, who brought so much joy and laughter to many people's lives, struggled with depression. Although he looked great on the outside, he was miserable deep down on the inside. Although outwardly he seemed to have a snappy answer and insights into people and current events, he did not have the internal insight necessary to keep from being overwhelmed by his personal pain. Although he hosted live shows and did interviews in which the funniest stuff he made up on the spot—a sign of magnificent intelligence—he did not know how to pull himself out from under the terrible weight of depression.

In the wake of Williams's suicide, actor, singer, entertainer, and TV host Wayne Brady, actor-comedian Chevy Chase, and many others have admitted they also struggle with the draining duffle bag of depression, doubt, and defeatism. In fact, more people than are willing to admit it have carried around this duffle bag of depression at one time or another in their lives. Many of us (yes, even us Christians) burden ourselves with the weight of this bag—a weight felt not in the shoulders but in the heart, robbing us of joy and plaguing us with sadness, sorrow, and gloom. We all have struggled with seasons in which the baggage of depression has held us down and threatened to suffocate us under its weight. Depression has

29

been defined as the common cold of the soul.

Depression is so much a part of life that if we search the Bible, we find many of the greatest biblical heroes also carried this baggage. Don't believe me? Let's take a look at several of them.

BIBLICAL HEROES CARRIED BAGGAGE, TOO

Job experienced the tremendous loss of his entire family, fortune, fame, and fitness, and he had a fluctuating faith. In fact, he said, "My days . . . come to an end without hope. My eyes will never see happiness again" (Job 7:6-7, NIV). That baggage of depression forced him to speak such lamentable language.

What about Moses? Moses was burdened with the responsibility of leading more than half a million people as they began their exodus from Egypt. He expressed his frustration and trepidation with the assignment God had given him in Deuteronomy 1:12: "How can I myself alone bear your cumbrance, and your burden, and your strife?" Moses did not know how he could carry the baggage of depression.

Then there was the great prophet Elijah. No one would expect him to have any troubles. The Bible says the power of God was so abundant with Elijah that—forget a private plane—he traveled in a whirlwind. Forget packing food, the birds fed him. Forget worrying about weather, he could make it rain, stop the rain, and even call down fire out of heaven through prayer. Yet in 1 Kings 19:4, after Jezebel, the personification of hell, threatened Elijah for killing the false prophets, he "went a day's journey into the wilderness, and came and sat down under a juniper tree: and he requested for himself that he might die; and said, It is enough; now, O LORD, take away my life; for I am not better than my fathers." Elijah carried the baggage of depression with him on his journey into the wilderness.

Still not convinced?

Consider King David who attempted to conceal his sin with Bathsheba. But it troubled him so much that he expressed, in poetic language in Psalm 32, that his spirit was groaning, and he felt he was under the heavy hand of God. On a later occasion, when he dealt with the rebellion and revolt of his son, Absalom, David prayed, "Oh, that I had the wings of a dove! I would fly away and be at rest" (Psalm 55:6, NIV). David certainly carried the bag of depression. So much so that he wanted to simply fly away from his burden.

Then there was Jeremiah, who was known throughout the Bible as the weeping prophet. He was so depressed that he actually cursed the day he was born. He declared in Jeremiah 20:14 (NIV), "Cursed be the day I was born! May the day my mother bore me not be blessed!"

Let's throw in one more for good measure: the prophet Jonah. Jonah was one of the first foreign missionaries—he worked with non-Jews. God told him to preach to the people of Nineveh, but Jonah didn't want to. He knew if he preached, they would repent. Instead, he wanted to see God punish them because he hated them. After he preached, they did indeed repent, but Jonah got so angry that he cried out to God, "Just kill me now, LORD! I'd rather be dead than alive if what I predicted will not happen" (Jonah 4:3, NLT). Jonah definitely carried the baggage of depression.

Depression is a common condition of being human and distresses most people at some time in their lives. Yet, even though so many people deal with it, most have no clear understanding of where depression comes from or why it is so pervasive.

There's a good reason we all experience depression: We all experience unfulfilled expectations, anger, and grief. Depression can be the emotional response that comes from the loss of something. It is an expression of grief turned inward, as with King David; or it is anger turned inward, as with Jonah. Emotional baggage of depression can get packed through experiencing death, illness, rejection, divorce, unemployment, abuse, transition, set back, lost relationships, or a plethora of other issues. There are countless trigger points for depression.

When we find ourselves in the throes of depression, we feel numb, exhausted, and detached. It feels as if a fog has rolled in over our hearts and we can't find our way. It throws off our emotional equilibrium. There's no joy, peace, or sense of serenity. It feels as if everything is completely out of sync.

All of these are the common symptoms of depression, yet it's important to know that not all depression is the same. Depression comes with different degrees of severity. Some cases of depression are mild to moderate and come as the result of dealing with the everyday pressures and difficulties of life.

The pendulum of depression, however, can swing from mild to moderate to severe, and some states of depression require medical and clinical attention. Unfortunately, there are believers who mistakenly believe something is wrong with your faith if you need clinical attention or medical assistance with your depression due to a chemical imbalance. Please understand that is simply untrue. In 2 Kings 20, when Hezekiah was ill, the prophet Isaiah told him that if he wanted to be healed, he needed to gather some figs, make a plaster, and put it on his sores. Isaiah's prescription to Hezekiah was for medicine.

Nowhere in Scripture does it indicate that something is lacking in your faith if you require medical attention, including medical attention for depression. More severe forms of depression are often caused by hormonal and chemical imbalances of neurotransmitters like serotonin. These balances can go wrong in people as easily as eyesight or hearing. No one would ever think something was spiritually wrong with a person who needed glasses or a hearing aid. Just as people need glasses to fix something wrong with their eyesight, others need serotonin inhibitors to regulate their chemical imbalances. Just as optometrists and ophthalmologists help with eyesight, trained clinical therapists and medical doctors have the ability to help people with depression as well.

If you feel you have a need for medical attention to escape the dark hole of depression, I encourage you to seek help from your medical doctor or therapist. For the purposes of this book, however, I am discussing moderate and mild forms of depression that come as a result of everyday pressures and challenges.

Unfortunately, some Christians minimize the misery of those who suffer with depression and act as if believers should never get depressed. Have you ever gone through something heavy and had some well-meaning friend try to spiritualize it or minimize it? They tell you, "You should have more faith" or "Didn't Paul say you should rejoice always?" or "Just get over it." Of course, if it were that easy, you would have done it already. Instead, let's look at Psalm 77 to glean principles designed to help us deal with this everyday depression that robs us of our joy, peace, and sense of optimism.

ASAPH'S DEPRESSION

Asaph wrote Psalm 77 during a time in which he was challenged by darkness, despair, and despondency. He did not waste time in getting to his point. In verses 1-2, he writes, "I cried unto God with my voice, even unto God with my voice; and he gave ear unto me. In the day of my trouble I sought the Lord: my sore ran in the night, and ceased not: my soul refused to be comforted."

Asaph was in distress. He was unable to find comfort or consolation because he was completely overwhelmed. Have you ever felt that way? Did you notice he felt this way even while he was praying to God? At times life can be so challenging that you cannot find comfort. You can spend the entire night praying, begging God to free you, to rescue you, to save you. In these times you can feel alone, but know that you are not. Not only is God with you in those times, but many others have experienced that place as well.

It is interesting to note what the psalmist did in this season of depression. Although he was feeling down, he mustered up enough spiritual fortitude to pray. He did not deny he was battling depression. He did not dodge it or pretend it did not exist. He did not bury his head in the sand of disillusionment or fake that he was happy.

We do that sometimes, don't we? We go through life smiling on the outside while we're miserable and depressed on the inside. Asaph, however, wasn't trying to fake it. Look at the intensity of his language: "I cried unto God with my voice, even unto God with my voice." He was depressed, but he prayed and sought after God in prayer. He didn't engage in escapist or self-destructive activities that would have resulted in him digging a deeper ditch for himself. Instead, he prayed.

Why?

Because other activities are only synthetic ways of dealing with the pains of life. You can go shopping and buy everything at your favorite stores; you can go to a restaurant and eat everything on the menu. But at the end of the day, after you've spent all your money, you may feel better for a moment, but the depression quickly seeps back in.

When we don't know how to deal with emotions in a healthy and positive way, we sometimes self-medicate. Studies show the massive abuse of drugs and alcohol around the world stems from the lack of dealing with emotions and problems in healthy, positive, and productive ways. In fact, the drugs people become addicted to work on the chemistry in the brain to help them to feel happier, to relax, to forget, and to feel numbed. But if you haven't dealt with the underlying problem, once you sober up, you're either right back where you started or even worse off. All these escapist forms of dealing with depression are unhealthy.

Let's look at what Asaph did and why he did it. Scripture says he prayed because he was a man of faith. Verse 3 says, "I remembered God, and was troubled: I complained, and my spirit was overwhelmed." This man of faith was so down that even his "thoughts of God" scared him. In other words, depression caused him to have a distorted view of God, which we will address shortly.

There are, in fact, three things in this text that indicate Asaph was depressed. This is not an exhaustive list of the symptoms of depression, but these three things are strong evidence of Asaph's depression and of ours as well. Verse 4 says, "Thou holdest mine eyes waking." This denotes *sleeplessness*. He was so depressed that he could not sleep. Moreover, he was so depressed that he blamed his sleeplessness on God. He said that God held his eyes open!

We sometimes feel this way when we are burdened and a myriad of questions bombard our minds such as: "God, why are You doing this to me? Why are You putting me through this? Why are You letting this happen?" We often blame God for our frustrations and issues, especially when we're tired and our minds don't have the energy to think clearly. Depression can interrupt our sleep patterns, and sometimes we end up in the opposite condition— sleeping too much. We don't want to wake up and face our miserable lives. We want to pull the covers over our heads and sleep and pretend the world isn't out there.

Look at the second part of verse 4: "I am so troubled that I cannot speak." He was so depressed that he couldn't even talk about it. He was both sleepless and *speechless*. He couldn't find the words to express what he felt. He couldn't articulate the agony or anguish of his disquieted soul. Do you ever feel that way? Someone asks you how you're doing or what's wrong, and you go blank. You can't think of words to verbalize the jumble of emotions assailing your heart and mind. Asaph wanted to rest, but he couldn't. He wanted to talk about it, but he couldn't.

And it got worse, but it also got better.

While he was on his Beautyrest® mattress trying to go to sleep, he remembered the old days when he used to sing a song to himself in the night. In verse 5, he says, "I have considered the days of old, the years of ancient times. I call to remembrance my song in the night: I commune with mine own heart: and my spirit made diligent search." He was a songwriter, remember? But Asaph, the songwriter, couldn't remember a single song to sing to make himself feel better. He was *songless*. Job 35:9-10 (NLT) says, "People cry out when they are oppressed. They groan beneath the power of the mighty. Yet they don't ask, 'Where is God my Creator, the one who gives songs in the night?' " Life had robbed Asaph of his song.

I don't know if you've ever been that depressed. Oftentimes, we live our lives and don't slow down enough to get in touch with our feelings. We do, however, notice our behavior has changed or see symptoms that worry us. You can't find any rest, so you start trying to figure out what's going on with you. You can't find the words to talk about it, or maybe you are scared to talk to other people about it. (After all, nowadays, if you confide something to someone, it's liable to end up on social media, so you keep it to yourself.) Or perhaps you imagine the only advice you get will be some empty platitude that leaves you more frustrated. You live in silent frustration. You remember when you used to be able to sing yourself out of this kind of stuff, but you can't even find a song to sing. How can this be?

In verse 3, Asaph says he "remembered God, and was troubled." What kind of thoughts did he recall about God?

ASAPH'S QUESTIONS
There are at least six different rhetorical questions Asaph posed of God, questions I believe give insight into why his thoughts of God troubled him.

The first question Asaph asked is in verse 7: "Will the Lord cast off forever?" As a songwriter, Asaph had some dissonant ideas or speculations about God. Here is his first dissonant speculation. He believed that God's presence had been retracted. He asked God if He had forgotten about him. Did God leave him there to fend for himself? Look at the finality of the word "forever." He didn't ask how many more days, weeks, or months before God would remember him—that would be bad enough. He asked if God had forgotten him *forever.*

The second question he asked is also found in verse 7: "Will he be favorable no more?" Again, there is finality in his thinking. He was not only worried about God's presence being retracted, but he was also concerned about God's pleasure being removed. He wondered if God lost a sense of pleasure in him so much so that God decided He would no longer be favorable toward him. Asaph concluded that God, for some undisclosed reason, became dissatisfied and utterly displeased with him to the extent that He no longer desired to bless him.

The third evidence of his dissonant speculation is in verse 8: "Is his mercy clean gone forever?" This time "forever" is in regards to God's mercy, His pardon. Asaph questioned God's benevolence to forgive. In other words, he was concerned that God's pardon had been recanted. Asaph wondered if he sinned in such a way that God's pardon was totally gone. He felt he had really blown it and was no longer a candidate for God's forgiveness and mercy.

Still, Asaph was not done yet. He went deeper. The second part of verse 8 asks, "Doth his promise fail forevermore?" He wondered if God's promises were reliable. He questioned all the promises God made and asked whether they fail forever. What about the promise God made in Psalm 34:9-10, "O fear the LORD, ye his saints: for there is no want to them that fear him. The young lions do lack, and suffer hunger: but they that seek the LORD shall not want any good thing"?

Has there ever been a moment in your life when you were so depressed that you started questioning God? Asaph was that depressed.

A fifth piece of evidence is found in verse 9: "Hath God forgotten to be gracious?" Had God's providence been rescinded?

Finally, in the second half of verse 9, he asked, "Hath he in anger shut up his tender mercies?" Had God's patience been reversed?

These verses point out that our depression and despondency can often be attributed directly to distorted views of God. Whether the distorted view of God brought on the negative thoughts or the depression caused his distorted view of God, can you see why Asaph's thoughts of God troubled him so much? The writer not only felt life was against him, but he also started to question whether God was against him as well.

> DEPRESSION AND DESPONDENCY CAN OFTEN BE ATTRIBUTED DIRECTLY TO DISTORTED VIEWS OF GOD.

If things ever get this desperate for you, here's something to remember: There is no question we can bring to God that will shake Him up. If I ever have a question that God is shaken by, then I have a problem with Him being my God, and that will never be so.

Asaph was so depressed that his whole perception of God was distorted. Does any of this feel familiar? You feel God has forgotten about you, that He doesn't love you anymore. You think He doesn't care because if He did, He wouldn't let you go through this. Like the disciple on the storm-tossed sea, you're asking, "Master, carest thou not?" (Mark 4:38).

Depression can work you over really well, can't it?

These things are the result of our minds reeling back and forth over the issues we're facing without knowing how to find focus and clarity. Think of it as an ocean storm tossing around a boat that has no anchor. When depression attacks our minds, we look for anything we can find to help stabilize our lives—one minute it's our fault, the next it's God's fault, then it's someone else's. Depression can leave us confused, top-heavy with the weight of its baggage and threatening to crash us into rocks, shipwrecking our lives.

ASAPH'S HANDLES

There is an amazing transition that takes place beginning in Psalm 77:10. Asaph gives us the first handle on the bag. We get to the good stuff—God's divine salvation. "And I said, This is my infirmity: but I will remember the years of the right hand of the most High. I will remember the works of the LORD: surely I will remember thy wonders of old" (Psalm 77:10-11).

Look at how Asaph experienced God's grace and power to save. There are at least four things Asaph does in the rest of this psalm that we can model to get free from depression. Notice that Asaph took action; he was intentional and purposeful in dealing with his depression. He did not sit around hoping and wishing his depression would go away. He took deliberate and focused action.

Our challenge, as expressed by Asaph, is simply, "Don't Forget to Remember." This challenge is paramount in that everyone from time to time tends to forget some things. As a case in point, according to Karen Bolla, a John Hopkins researcher, forgetfulness is a common plight of humanity. These are the things people most often forget:

1. Names: 83 percent
2. Where something is: 60 percent
3. Telephone numbers: 57 percent
4. Words: 53 percent
5. What was said: 49 percent
6. Faces: 42 percent
7. Whether or not you've just done something: 38 percent[2]

However, there are some things we need to remember to forget because they can become emotional baggage of the past. Conversely, there are other things we must not forget to remember, namely the past performances of God according to Asaph.

The first thing we must remember is God's past performance. Asaph said, "Yes, I'm depressed; I'm overwhelmed. I'm going through a rough and tough season in my life. I'm going through a moment of despair and despondency. I'm dealing with an infirmity. But, God, I will remember Your past performance." Asaph looked in the rearview mirror of his life to God's past performance. He chose not to suffer from a case of convenient amnesia. This wasn't his first time dealing with life's difficulties. It was as if he was saying "I've been here before!"

Likewise, look over your past and say as he did, "This isn't the first time someone has walked out of my life. This isn't the first time I've been unemployed. This isn't the first time I've gotten a negative report from my doctor or my supervisor. This isn't the first time I've been rejected. This isn't the first time I've seen dark and difficult days. God, if You showed up and performed in my life in the past, if You were able to demonstrate Your love and grace in the past, then I'm not sweating what's going on in my life right now."

You must remember not to forget His past performances in your life. Look back over the many dangerous toils and snares you've already overcome. The same God who kept you in the past is the same God who keeps you now.

Asaph continued in Psalm 77:11, "I will remember the works of the LORD." The second thing he says follows closely behind in verse 10: "Surely I will remember thy wonders of old."

There is a difference between God's works and His wonders. "His wonders" denote the unprecedented performances of God. "His works" denote the day-to-day blessings God performs. The wonders are the things that blow your mind. The wonders are those "nothing and nobody-but-God" moments, things that only God could pull off.

For instance, you should have some bookmarks in your life. Like with your Bible or this book you're reading now, you may put a bookmark at a point where you last stopped reading so you can remember to go back to that point. You might also put bookmarks in other places where you found encouragement, something you wanted to share, or places where God touched your heart. As in a good book or in your Bible, you also need to have some book-marks set in your life on a few of God's works and others set on a few of His wonders.

The fact that you're able to read this book right now is one of God's works for you. Do you know over 775 million adults world-wide cannot read? In the United States, more than 32 million people have below-basic literacy skills.[3] Just being able to read these words is something to thank God for. You were born in a country with schools you can go to and learn to read. You had someone who made sure you went to school. That's a work of God. You have eyes that function and a brain that thinks and comprehends—these are both wonders and works of God.

In Psalm 77:11, Asaph said he was going to start with remembering all of these things. He was going to exercise his mind to focus on the blessings he had received throughout his entire life rather than the stuff that happened to be going wrong at the moment. That's a powerful tool for us to use, too. We need to be deliberate and be intentional in focusing our minds on God's works and wonders if we want to get a grip on the draining duffle bag of depression, doubt, and defeatism.

Paul instructs us to have a transcendent thought life: "Finally, brethren, whatsoever things are true, whatsoever things are honest, whatsoever things are just, whatsoever things are pure, whatsoever things are lovely, whatsoever things are of good report; if there be any virtue, and if there be any praise, think on these things" (Philippians 4:8).

You have to remember God's past performances, but you also have to reflect on God's phenomenal provisions. So many people have the testimony of the doctor who said he'd done all he could do, but then God showed up and did a little bit more. In other words, God pulled off something extraordinary that no one else could have done.

If there's ever been a time in your life where you fell on your knees and thanked God for something He did for you, you should have a bookmark on that moment as well. I'm not talking about the time you prayed for a parking spot close to the store and got one. I'm talking about the time you lost control of your car and miraculously avoided a horrible accident or the time you had a horrible accident and miraculously survived by the grace of God or the time you walked into some place you should not have been and made it out alive. Asaph remembered these things, too.

Perhaps you are still perplexed regarding what exactly you should remember as it pertains to God's intervention in your life. Here are a few things the Bible expresses that God's people were to remember. These will serve us well to remember, as well.

- The deliverance the Lord has wrought (Deuteronomy 5:15)
- The way God has led (Deuteronomy 8:2)
- The blessings God has bestowed

(Deuteronomy 32:7-12)
- The victories God has won (Deuteronomy 11:2-7)
- The encouragement God has given (Joshua 23:14)

David said it this way: "Some trust in chariots, and some in horses," which is another way of saying that some people rely on their own resources (Psalm 20:7). Then David added, "But we will remember the name of the LORD our God."

Do you remember God's phenomenal provisions in your life, or do you take His goodness for granted? How many deliverances, blessings, and victories can you name right now that God has provided for you? Take a moment to thank God for all of those times in your life.

If you want to deal with your depression, there has to be a depth of intentionality. "I will," Asaph said. "I'm not going to have a pity party. I'm not going to have a defeatist mentality. I'm not going to let the devil continue to talk me out of my future and my destiny. *I will* remember God's past performance. *I will* reflect on his phenomenal provision, but I'm also going to report His purposeful providence."

Verse 12 says, "I will meditate also of all thy work, and talk of thy doings." In other words, stop talking about what's *not working* in your life, and start talking about how God *is working* in your life. As a matter of fact, Asaph kept talking about what God was doing and what he believed God was going to do until he talked himself out of depression. That is partly what encouraging yourself in the Lord means. Sometimes you have to talk to yourself.

Remember the story of the woman with the issue of blood? Before she was healed, she said to herself, "If I may but touch his garment" (Matthew 9:21). She hadn't yet touched Jesus' hem, but she told herself, "If I could just get close enough to sneak a touch, I know I will be made whole."

Like that woman, you've got to learn to talk to yourself, reason with yourself, and tell yourself you're not going to spend another night being depressed. How? Talk about what God has done, is doing, and will do in your life. Talk about what you expect Him to do in your life. Speak with the language of victory and faith. "I'm coming out of this. I'm going to be the head and not the tail. My best days are ahead. I'm going with God all the way!" Learn how to talk yourself out of the depressing stuff that has you bound, as Asaph did.

If you want to get out of your depression, you have to rethink the preeminence of God's person. Look at Psalm 77:13: "Thy way, O God, is in the sanctuary: who is so great a God as our God?" What happened to Asaph? He started off with the distorted perception of God, but by the time he finished talking to himself, he had a whole new attitude. At first he questioned God, but then he resolved to spend some time in worship. After he went into the sanctuary—better yet, he entered into the presence of God—he spent time with God and had a totally different view of God.

Asaph thought about all the doors God had opened, all the ways He had made, all the times He miraculously showed up in his life, all the times He delivered him. Then Asaph said, "Now I have a question for myself—who is greater than our God?" Asaph recounted God's deeds. He said God kept the Israelites when they came out of bondage. He allowed them to walk through the Red Sea. Asaph said that if God could keep them through that, He could certainly keep him through what he was going through right then.

Tell yourself that you are not going to spend any more time, energy, or effort being depressed over something God can change whenever He decides to change it. The reality of your life is that God supernaturally supervises your season of sorrow and suffering, and He is able to bring you out with His mighty hand.

What this passage in Psalms clearly shows us is that worship recalibrates the soul. Even if your circumstances do not change, worship will change *you* so that you can embrace whatever the circumstance is and still be able to testify that God is good. Asaph transitioned from a point of questioning God to declaring his confidence in God.

How?

By worshiping.

Worship can only happen when we acknowledge God's power, adore God's presence, attest to God's person, and admit to God's preeminence. Asaph didn't go to church as we know it in the twenty-first century, but he connected with God through the practice outlined here.

Worship that moves the heart of God is always personally experienced before it is publically expressed. Once Asaph refocused his mind and intention on God, his attitude and energy shifted. This isn't about going to church, although that can be critical in focusing your mind and attention on God—His greatness, His goodness, His love, His control over your life, and His peace. Some people believe that in order to worship God they have to be in church somewhere, but the truth is that your worship has to be mobile. Your worship has to be like your cell phone—wherever you are, it's there with you. Wherever you are, you can connect with God.

> WORSHIP CAN ONLY HAPPEN WHEN WE ACKNOWLEDGE GOD'S POWER, ADORE GOD'S PRESENCE, ATTEST TO GOD'S PERSON, AND ADMIT TO GOD'S PREEMINENCE.

Beware of a worship that is geographically restricted to a particular location. The woman at Jacob's well had this misconception of worship, as she declared to Jesus in John 4:19-20. After having her morally dubious past exposed by Jesus regarding her five husbands and her recent live-in partner, she said to Jesus, "Sir, I perceive that thou art a prophet." Being in the "hot seat" regarding her sins, the woman shifted the conversation to worship by stating, "Our Fathers worshipped in this mountain; and ye say that in Jerusalem is the place where men ought to worship."

Can you see how she and those in her day ascribed to ideology of worship that was geographically restricted? To which Jesus responded, "Woman, believe me, the hour cometh, when ye shall neither in this mountain, nor yet at Jerusalem, worship the Father. Ye worship ye know not what: we know what we worship: for salvation is of the Jews. But the hour cometh, and now is, when the true worshippers shall worship the Father in spirit and in truth: for the Father seeketh such to worship Him. God is a Spirit: and they that worship him, must worship him in spirit and in truth."

The communal gathering of believers is critically important and exhorted in Scripture. Yet we must understand, as Asaph did, that genuine worship is a matter of one's heart before God and not merely a place.

PANACEA FOR DEPRESSION

I want to confess something. As you read this, if it seems like I know a lot about this topic of depression, it's because I do. I've been there, done that. In fact, I'm prone to slip back into depression every now and then if I don't catch myself every. My wife will tell you there are moments and seasons in my life when I do not want to talk. Things overwhelm me sometimes, even as a pastor. Yes, even pastors can slip into that dark place of depression.

Please don't judge me. No one is exempt or excused from the possibility of depression. Sometimes things can rock your world and shake you into a state of emotional vulnerability. I was so depressed many years ago that I thought life wasn't worth living, and I wanted to slip into oblivion somewhere as I suffered from suicidal thoughts. Even though this was quite a while ago, I'll never forget it.

I preached a sermon from Psalm 42 called "Panacea for Depression." (Not every sermon a pastor preaches is for his congregation. That sermon was for me.) I was going through a tough season of my life, and I started having distorted thoughts about God, such as, "God, You forgot me. You don't care about me. You don't love me. I can't be of any use to You." Whenever you allow Satan to suggest those types of thoughts, your thinking will become distorted. I started thinking I might as well check out of here. But here's the lesson: That was one little season.

One moment I decided to read my Bible and, as God would have it, the Scripture I opened to was 1 Kings 19:1-4 (the verse I mentioned earlier that recounts the time Elijah wanted to kill himself). I was in one of my counseling classes and heard a counselor say, "Suicide is a permanent solution to a temporary problem." Whatever you go through on this earth is temporary, but suicide is permanent. Those words at that emotional vulnerable season of my life gave me the hope I needed to press on.

We talked about letting go of baggage. I don't want you to think there is anything wrong with you if you've been carrying the draining duffle bag of depression, doubt, and defeatism. Don't fret, because depression is part of life. We all face seasons when life becomes overwhelming. When the pain becomes acute, we sometimes question whether we have what it takes to get through it. I pray you are more encouraged than ever before. You're going to get through whatever you may be dealing with. God is on your side! But it's going to take some intention on your part; you have to be deliberate about fighting depression. You must have dogmatic determination. Like Asaph, you can say, "I will remember His past works. I will remember what He's doing right now. And I'm going to talk about it even if people call me a fanatic. No matter what, I'm going to keep reminding myself how good God is." Don't forget to remember!

If you or someone you know suffers from depression, here is my prayer for you and a prayer you can pray to God:

> *Dear Father,*
>
> *We acknowledge, confess, and admit that the heavy bags of depression are hanging on our hearts. Some of us have experienced a loss of loved ones. Others, a season of transition. Some, a relationship that has been ruptured. Others are dealing with the day-to-day pressures of trying to keep all the balls of life juggling at one time. Father, You know how we're overwhelmed. Some of us have not been able to sleep; others of us are trying to sleep the misery*

away. We want to talk, but we don't know who to talk to. We don't trust our pains with just anybody, so we're speechless. So Father, first of all, we ask You to forgive us—for the times that we couldn't see You clearly, the times we questioned You, the times we had distorted views of You, the times we didn't think You cared about us or loved us, the times we thought we had blown it so badly that You decided to take Your hands off of us. We come against every thought of the wicked one who seeks to sow seeds of doubt, discouragement, and defeat in us. We bring every thought down into captivity of the knowledge of Christ so that dark thoughts should never live in our minds. We trust Your love, Your character. We thank You for Your mercies. Father, we now ask You to renew us. Give us enough grace to get through the day-to-day challenges. We ask that You give us the power, the stamina, and the grace we need. Father, help us to remember how You've moved in the past, how You've made a way, how You've opened doors. Give us clear recall of not just Your works, but also Your wonders. Remind us of the miracles in our lives that only You could execute. Change our orientation even now. You are a great God, and You are greatly to be praised. We thank You for our destiny. Thank You now for our future. Thank You that brighter days are ahead. Thank You for restoring of our joy and our confidence. Thank You for renewing our faith today. And to that end, Father, we resolve to praise You. We bless Your name.

In Jesus' name. Amen.

CHAPTER TWO
The Agonizing Attaché Case of Anxiety

"Take therefore no thought for the morrow: for the morrow shall take thought for the things of itself. Sufficient unto the day is the evil thereof."
(Matthew 6:34)

Near the end of 1999, the entire country was preparing for the stroke of midnight and the beginning of the new millennium. Prior to 2000, the news carried the story of the dreaded Y2K computer crisis, a phenomenon the world had never dealt with before. It was the first time computers that ran the banking systems, electrical grids, oil pipelines, traffic, overseas shipping logistics, and security systems of the world had to deal with a century other than 1900. Since all computers were built in the 1900's and it was helpful to save computer memory wherever possible, many programs were designed to use only two digits to indicate the year. Now they would need four digits.

It was rumored that computers around the world might accidentally confuse the turning of the year from '99 to '00 (meaning 1900, not 2000) and accidentally delete everything—all financial transactions, all money in banks, all credit records, all tax records (some of those wouldn't be so bad). All electronic information that existed would vanish. Furthermore, electricity would shut off, gas would stop flowing, millions of packages would be lost, phone systems would shut down, and planes would fall from the sky. Chaos would ensue all over the world. We would be thrown back into the dark ages of paper and typewriters, while librarians and archivists worked with techies to figure out where all the information was stored and how to retrieve it.

Entire companies sprang up dedicated to ensure Y2K safety. Specialists were hired, new computer systems were built, and billions of dollars were spent trying to make sure Y2K was not the end of the world. As the clock struck midnight, people in America were anxious, even though nothing had happened anywhere else in the world.

It was all for nothing. There were computer glitches, but the large corporations were proactive and therefore ready for the new millennium, so most people saw no impact. Some smaller companies had problems, but they resolved them fairly quickly. All the mass hysteria was pointless.

Such is the nature of anxiety.

AN EPIDEMIC

I'm going to guess that you are familiar with the emotional baggage of anxiety. Most everyone is familiar with anxiety; it is a problem of epidemic proportions. Perhaps you know it better by its more common name: worry. Worry and anxiety are so common in our society that we see their impact on our lives, both mentally and physically. All of us have had times in our lives when we've found ourselves so preoccupied with concerns that we've started to worry. It's been said that our present age is the age of anxiety. It seems as if everyone is anxious about something. It's hard to prevent it, but by the grace of God, we'll find solutions in the next few pages.

Years ago, most people were only concerned with the things that happened around themselves and their families. If things were well in the village, then things were well in the world. News that happened in far-off lands rarely came to their attention in their entire lifetimes. However, since the advent of television, satellites, international news reporting, and other social media outlets such as Twitter, Facebook, and YouTube, we see things happening all over the world the moment they happen. Atrocities people used to only learn about if the story made it to print (and if they had the time and the desire to read a newspaper or a history book), now come directly to us via our mobile phones in real time and in vivid HD color.

It's hard not to succumb to worry and anxiety when so much information floods our daily lives. Yet, as prevalent as it is, being anxious or worried is one of the most counterproductive things we can do. In fact, it has been said that worry is like a rocking chair: It will give you something to do, but it won't get you anywhere. You can put a lot of effort into it, but it doesn't achieve anything.

> **BEING ANXIOUS OR WORRIED IS ONE OF THE MOST COUNTERPRODUCTIVE THINGS WE CAN DO.**

The word *worry* comes from the Old English word *wyrgan*, which means to strangle or seize by the throat. A simple definition would be excessive concern over the affairs of life. The key word is *excessive*. Anxiety happens when you are so focused on the problems of life that you can think of nothing else. It is an all-consuming feeling of uncertainty, fear, and pessimism.

LEGITIMATE WORRY

I want to look at anxiety from two perspectives. First, there is a legitimate form of anxiety we can call "concern." An example of legitimate concern, which is natural and would create tension, is failure to study for an exam you have tomorrow morning. In that situation, you have a legitimate reason to be worried because you've failed to prepare yourself for something you knew was coming. There is a reason or rationale to that worry. That's not the kind of worry I want to deal with in this chapter. I want to deal with the form of worry that Jesus spoke about in Matthew 6:25-34. It opposes the life of faith that Jesus wants us to live.

Let's examine three aspects of illegitimate worry. First, the type of worry that is illegitimate is one that is irreverent. Worry is irreverent when it fails to recognize God as the Source and Sustainer of our lives. Worry causes us to bring into question the wisdom, power, and ways of God, which are all acts of mistrust.

When we become so preoccupied with the problems and perplexities of our lives that we no longer recognize God as sovereign, worry can cause us to enter a place of doubt where we no longer place our faith in God. In fact, we do the opposite: Our trust is no longer in God's hands; it's in our own. Worry can cause us to lose sight of God's sovereign hand, which results in seeing life as a complete accident as opposed to seeing the events of life in the light of God's appointment.

In addition to the illegitimate form of worry being irreverent, it is also irrelevant. In most cases, we find that when we face something that causes us to worry, we have no way to control it. So all the worry is pointless. All the effort and energy we employ to address the cause of the worry is to no avail because worry does not change the reality of the situation. You can be filled with anxiety and worry all night long. But guess what? The next morning, the thing you worried about is still there. Worry never reverses our circumstances and situations. Worry tends to magnify our problems.

Another aspect of the illegitimate worry Jesus wants us to avoid is that it is irresponsible. Why? Because it is counterproductive to the way we should address our problems. We end up spending more mental energy than we ought to spend worrying, rather than researching and coming up with the proper solution or applying the proper discipline to resolve the issue.

In Matthew 6:25-34, in one of his best known sermons, commonly known as "The Sermon on the Mount," Jesus poignantly discusses worry and tells us multiple times not to take thought of our lives, not to be anxious about our lives, and not to be preoccupied with the problems of our lives to the degree that we find ourselves no longer trusting God. Jesus shares six problems with anxiety.

PROBLEMS WITH ANXIETY

First, anxiety will exasperate our feelings. Anxiety, in this sense, is akin to depression, which we discussed in the last chapter. Anxiety opens the door to depression because it can so fill you with a sense of worry that you no longer trust God. Once you lose trust in God, your emotions are vulnerable to attack. Worry exasperates your feelings. In other words, worry can make us emotional wrecks.

Second, in Matthew 6:27, Jesus teaches that anxiety is an exercise in futility. He posed the question, "How many of you in the process of being full of anxiety have been able to add even a cubit to your stature?" The phrase "cubit to your stature" has been interpreted different ways. One interpretation is to worry yourself into a growth spurt. It simply doesn't happen that way. The other way to interpret is to add a single day to the length of your life by worrying about it. The reality is that worry does the opposite of that. Rather than adding days to your life, worry can take away days and years from your life. There is no positive outcome that ever emerges from worry or anxiety. In fact, worry can adversely affect your blood pressure and heart rate and cause headaches, which can be physically and psychologically damaging.

Third, Jesus teaches us that anxiety will exaggerate the future. Most anxiety is linked to anticipated situations that rarely ever happen. You find yourself worrying about stuff that not only hasn't happened yet but most likely won't ever happen. Things are rarely as bad as we imagine them to be. As a result, many of us crucify ourselves between two thieves: regret of yesterday on one side and worry of tomorrow on the other.

In the book *The Screwtape Letters*, C. S. Lewis introduces us to a fictional senior demon named Screwtape who is advising his nephew, a junior demon, on how best to control people and make them ineffective. Screwtape tells his nephew that the great secret of demons is to keep humans looking either forward to an uncertain future or backward at a life of regret. Either way works the same, he suggests. The key is never to let them live in the present because the present is the only thing they really have.

Life can be hard and difficult to deal with, but when you worry you assume an even more difficult life tomorrow that has not yet happened. Jesus says you've got enough stuff to deal with today, so why try to load up with tomorrow's stuff, too?

Fourth, worry exhibits faithlessness. In verse 30, Jesus asked, "Wherefore, if God so clothe the grass of the field, which today is, and tomorrow is cast into the oven, shall he not much more clothe you, O ye of little faith?" Jesus chided His disciples for having an anemic faith. Look at the indictment in that verse. Jesus explains the reason you are full of anxiety is because you are not full of faith. As God, He's saying, "If I'm competent and capable enough to see to it that the grounds are covered with grass and the birds have food to eat and don't have to go out and work for it, can't you trust me enough to take care of you? When you allow anxiety to enter your heart, it exhibits your faithlessness."

Anxiety says, "God, I really don't trust You. I really don't believe You have everything under control, and so I feel like I have to take things into my own hands. But because my hands are so weak and feeble, and I know my tendency to mess things up when they're in my hands, I'm now full of worry and anxiety."

Fifth, anxiety will eclipse our focus. In verse 33, Jesus says, "But seek ye first the kingdom of God, and his righteousness; and all these things shall be added unto you." The command implies that if you are worried, you are unable to focus on and seek God's kingdom. Perhaps you haven't been seeking His kingdom because you've been too worried about trying to build your own kingdom. Jesus says when you are full of anxiety, you lose all sense of kingdom focus. When you're focused on building your own kingdom and things aren't lining up in your kingdom, suddenly you get anxious. This happens because you've taken your eyes off advancing God's kingdom. His kingdom is no longer a priority in your life because it's been eclipsed by anxiety.

Do you understand how an eclipse works? The earth revolves around the sun, and the moon revolves around the earth. The moon is held by the earth's orbit; the earth is held by the sun's orbit. The reason they are held this way is because the sun is 1,300,000 times the size of the earth. Similarly, the earth is four times the size of the moon. Actually, the moon is about the same size as the continent of Asia. This means the sun is 5,200,000 times the size of the moon.

The earth needs the sun to live. The sun does not need the earth. Without the sun, there'd be no life on earth. Every so often the moon moves between the sun and the earth. Since the moon is closer to the earth, it can block out the light of the sun, even though the sun is over five million times the size of the moon.

That's how it is when you let your own little kingdom fill your mind and get in the way: You can actually block out God's much bigger, much brighter kingdom. But what we need is God's kingdom, not our own kingdom. Our kingdom, like the moon, is a barren rock. The Son, namely "The Son of God," is like the sun and is the life-giving power for us. Worry eclipses our focus and darkens our world.

Finally, anxiety expends our fuel. Have you ever noticed that when you are full of worry, you are also the most weak? Worry comes with an enormous price. It costs a lot emotionally, mentally, physically, and spiritually. Worry produces the stress hormone cortisol, which is responsible for accumulating fat around your midsection, and fat around the midsection is a leading cause of heart disease. When you sit around worrying, you'll feel drained and depleted. It strangles the life out of you. Worry can have you driving on fumes and ultimately leave you stranded on the road of life.

Many times, however, God put you in that situation, not to abandon you but to test your trust, refuel your faith, and strengthen your resolve. The apostle Paul spoke of the troubles in his life at a strategic moment that tested his capacity to trust God. Paul declared, "For we would not, brethren, have you ignorant of our trouble which came to us in Asia, that we were pressed out of measure, above strength, insomuch that we despaired even of life: But we had the sentence of death in ourselves, that we should not trust in ourselves, but in God which raiseth the dead: who delivered us from so great a death, and doth deliver: in whom we trust that he will yet deliver us" (2 Corinthians 1:8-10).

However, instead of trusting, we often take things into our small, feeble hands and try to burn the candle at both ends because we're worried about keeping it all together. But God is sitting in your corner, waiting on you to trust Him. Hasn't He proven himself to you enough? Hasn't He shown you He can handle things? Look at the birds, He says. None of them are stressing or worrying like you. In fact, they're singing!

Verse 31 says, "Therefore take no thought, saying, What shall we eat? or, What shall we drink? or, Wherewithal shall we be clothed?" Remember, David said in Psalm 37:25, "I have been young, and now am old; yet have I not seen the righteous forsaken, nor his seed begging bread." Isn't it true?

Perhaps you or someone you know has the testimony of being unemployed. If you're like the people I know, you didn't lose one pound while you were unemployed. Why? Because God saw to it that you had food. He made sure you had something to drink. Jesus says not to worry about fashion, about the symbols of success that make people pay attention to you. You're worried about the label in the back of your shirt, and you can't even enjoy life because you have been walking around with this heavy attaché case of anxiety.

POCKETS OF ANXIETY

Attaché cases have a big section in the middle and a bunch of little pockets. That's how anxiety works on you. There's often one big thing that causes worry and a bunch of little things that go along with it. But here's the secret: Most of the stuff you're worrying about is all in your imagination. That's why Jesus says three times in this passage (in verses 27, 28, and 34) to "take no thought." Stop listening to Satan tell you that things won't get better. Stop spending time worrying about what's wrong. Stop filling your mind with anxious thoughts. Our thoughts are the culprit behind worry, fabricating a world of pessimism and defeat.

We have to use proper hermeneutics, or methods of interpretation, to get the fullest meaning of this text. One principle of hermeneutics is that whenever you see a "therefore," go back one verse and see what it's "there for." That is, go back and study the immediate context. Since this passage we're studying begins in verse 25 with "Therefore," we need to go back to verse 24. Interestingly enough, Jesus says in verse 24, "No man can serve two masters: for either he will hate the one, and love the other; or else he will hold to the one, and despise the other. Ye cannot serve God and mammon."

Mammon is money. Jesus said when you begin to serve money, you will be anxious and always worry about stuff. When money becomes the center of your joy and the focus of your attention, anxiety will fill your life. Take inventory of your worries now. How much of your worry is financially based?

PRESCRIPTIONS FOR ANXIETY

So how do we deal with anxiety? We understand the problem, but now we want to understand the solution. Let's look at the answers Jesus gives us.

The first prescription for anxiety is to rely on the providence of God. Instead of worrying, we should trust that God will provide for us and will protect us. This is the underlying theme of Matthew 6:25-34. Jesus repeatedly told His disciples that He would take care of them.

Look at verse 25-26 again. Jesus says, "Take no thought for your life, what ye shall eat, or what ye shall drink; nor yet for your body, what ye shall put on. Is not the life more than meat, and the body than raiment? Behold the fowls of the air: for they sow not, neither do they reap, nor gather into barns; yet your heavenly Father feedeth them. Are ye not much better than they?" In these verses, Jesus makes a point about the reliability of God. You can rely on His providential care.

I also want to make a point here so that these verses are not misunderstood. Relying on God does not negate human responsibility and preparation. Jesus says the birds are not full of anxiety. They are not worrying. "For they sow not, neither do they reap, nor gather into barns; yet your heavenly Father feedeth them." Understand, though, that a bird is not idle. A bird doesn't sit around waiting on food to come. God says He will provide, but His provision involves your participation.

The Bible also says that a man who will not work ought not to eat (2 Thessalonians 3:10). You run the risk of going hungry if you refuse to be responsible enough to prepare and participate in the process of being gainfully employed. An erroneous theological concept suggests that blessings fall from the sky without our involvement. Birds have enough faith and trust that when they get up in the morning, God is going to have some seeds or worms for them; they just have to get up and go find them. The seeds aren't going to the birds. The birds have to do their part; use what God gave them; and fly to find the lizards, berries, insects, and seeds. Likewise, we have responsibility to be fully engaged on our end as well.

The second prescription for anxiety is to remain in the present with God. This means you should spend no time living in the past or rushing ahead of God by living in the unknown future. Living between these two extremes produces constant anxiety. In Matthew 6:34, Jesus says, "Take therefore no thought for the morrow: for the morrow shall take thought for the things of itself. Sufficient unto the day is the evil thereof." In other words, each day has enough trouble of its own. God does not promise that our days will be free of trouble. When we worry about tomorrow, we add to the troubles of today. There's enough trouble in today that you don't need to add tomorrow's trouble to it, too. One has wisely stated, "Don't miss the sun today worrying about the rain coming tomorrow."

Jesus says to remain in the present. That does not mean, however, that you do not plan. Rather, it means you plan in pencil. Don't write your plans in ink, because your plans are always subject to change. God honors your preparation, provided you give Him freedom to change what you prepared.

There is a truth you must understand about God's daily provisions. He told Paul, "My grace is sufficient for thee" (2 Corinthians 12:9). God gives His provision each day, as we need it. Lamentations 3:23 says that God's compassions "are new every morning: great is thy faithfulness." Deuteronomy 33:25 says, "As thy days, so shall thy strength be."

Remember, when the Israelites were in the desert, God gave them manna from heaven every morning. When some tried to gather it up to store for later, it rotted. God wanted them to trust His provision for that day. Whatever the day's need is, God will give you the strength to meet it. He didn't promise tomorrow's grace today. When tomorrow arrives, there will be new stuff to deal with as well as new strength and grace to deal with it. Corrie Ten Boom, who survived the Nazi Holocaust and helped countless Jews escape during World War II, said it best: "Worrying does not empty tomorrow of its troubles, it empties today of its strength."[4]

The third prescription for anxiety is to respond in prayer to God. The apostle Paul, in Philippians 4:6, says, "Be anxious for nothing, but in everything by prayer and supplication with thanksgiving let your requests be made known to God" (NASB). You won't be anxious if you're praying about everything because you're responding in prayer to the things that would typically cause you to worry. You are giving your worries and problems to God. And He says do it with thanksgiving. This may sound paradoxical, but God wants you to have enough faith not only to pray believing He will hear and answer your prayer but also to thank God before He even does what you ask—before the outcome is manifest, before the victory comes, before the door opens! You must have enough faith to praise God regardless of what He decides to do.

God says to "let your request be made known." When you tell God your request, He has several options as a response: He can do what you ask; He can deny what you ask; or He can delay what you ask. Remember, you are making a request, not giving God a command. Regardless of what God decides to do, you have to embrace His decision. He always has our best interests in mind. You must get to the place in your faith where your attitude is, "God, whether You do it, deny it, or delay it, I'm good. I trust You either way because I know it's all for my good. So I'm going to praise You in advance of Your decision."

First Peter 5:7 says, "Casting all your care upon him; for he careth for you." The word *cast* actually means "to toss." Peter says to take all those things that are weighing you down—that entire attaché case of anxiety—and toss it on God because He cares for you. God wants you to toss Him the things you can't handle; and when you do, don't try to take it back out of His hands. Trust Him to work it out. Then you're traveling lighter. In fact, Paul says in Philippians 4:7, that when you give your anxieties to God, "the peace of God, which surpasses all comprehension, will guard your hearts and your minds in Christ Jesus" (NASB).

"Peace that passes all understanding" means you won't even be able to understand the sense of serenity you have. Even in the face of tremendous circumstances, you will have peace. When you place your full confidence in God, there is a deep sense of assurance that everything will work out for your good. Why? Because you know He will keep your heart and mind through Christ Jesus. The word *keep* means "to guard." In other words, God will set up a supernatural garrison (or military fort) to protect you.

God will put your heart and mind under divine protection so that the stuff around you won't affect you as usual. If you're not praying, you're out there fending for yourself with no protection or reinforcement. Prayer acknowledges your weakness and your willingness to seek help from someone greater than yourself. As a result of your prayer, God places a garrison around your heart and mind to you keep you in peace. People won't understand why you're not falling apart. You may even have trouble understanding why you're not falling apart. It is God guarding and keeping you.

Isaiah 26:3 says God "wilt keep him in perfect peace, whose mind is stayed on thee: because he trusteth in thee." When you think about God instead of your problems, God will keep you in peace. When you think about how good God has been, how He's opened doors, blessed you, healed you, given you victory, you will have His perfect peace.

The fourth prescription for anxiety is to realign your priority to

God. In Matthew 6:31-34, Jesus says, "Therefore take no thought, saying, What shall we eat? or, What shall we drink? or, Wherewithal shall we be clothed? (For after all these things do the Gentiles seek:) for your heavenly Father knoweth that ye have need of all these things. But seek ye first the kingdom of God, and his right-eousness; and all these things shall be added unto you." Jesus an-chors His whole teaching on anxiety with this section by saying you have to realign your priorities to God. He juxtaposes being filled with anxiety and seeking first the kingdom of God by saying that worrying over things is how unbelievers live; it's not the way be-lievers are to live or operate in God's kingdom.

Unbelievers do not have a kingdom consciousness. Jesus says that believers must "seek first" the kingdom of God. The kingdom of God means the comprehensive reign and rule of God in our lives. If worry has inundated your life, perhaps you have let some-thing else become a priority for you other than God's kingdom. Realign your priorities until you are paying most attention to God's kingdom as you pursue His righteousness. Jesus says all the other mundane matters or carnal concerns you've been worrying about will be met if you make God your priority.

How do you make God your priority? Jesus says to recognize the reign of the King. Recognize that you are not in charge—God is. Most worry and anxiety comes from our wanting to be in con-trol; and once life is spinning out of control, we become anxious and worried. When we want to be in control and are not, we feel anxious. But when Jesus says to seek first God's kingdom, He wants you to recognize that God is the One in charge. He reigns. You're not the one on the throne—He is.

Here's the benefit of this mindset: Once you recognize the reign of the King, you can access the resources from His kingdom. A king's responsibility is to take care of those who live under his do-main. As the King of kings, God provides for those who are sub-jects under His sovereignty. So the worse mistake we can make is to decide we want to build our kingdom at the expense of building His kingdom. When you seek God's kingdom and His righteousness, He makes sure the other things you need are added to your life as well. Seeking His righteousness means you're not only seeking after mere gold, honor, or praise.

What is God's righteousness? Micah 6:8 says, God "hath shewed thee, O man, what is good; and what doth the LORD require of thee, but to do justly, and to love mercy, and to walk humbly with thy God?" When you're practicing these things in your life, you become a conduit through which those around you can see the resources and benefits of God's kingdom. His righteousness should be evident in the way you walk and talk, in your manner of living. When you focus on His kingdom and diligently pursue His righteousness, God says He's got everything else covered. And by everything else, God means your needs, not your greeds. Often the things we worry about are the stuff we want rather than our true needs.

So the prescription for dealing with anxiety is, first, to rely on the providence of God. He's taking care of the birds and can most certainly take care of you. Second, remain in the present with God, not the past or the future. Train your mind to stay in the present, and don't let it wander into next week or ahead of God. The only time that really exists is the present. The past is gone, and the future is not promised. Third, respond in prayer to God. Let God know what's troubling you so He can guard your heart and mind. Fourth, realign your priority to God. Recognize the reign of the King; then you will receive the resources of His kingdom.

Anxiety does not need to be part of your life. Jesus came to give us life and give it more abundantly. He didn't come so that we would live like the rest of the world. This may be the age of anxiety, but we are not the people of anxiety, and our God is not a god of anxiety and fear. God does not pace the floor. He does not fret or sit in heaven

> THIS MAY BE THE AGE OF ANXIETY, BUT WE ARE NOT THE PEOPLE OF ANXIETY, AND OUR GOD IS NOT A GOD OF ANXIETY AND FEAR.

twiddling His thumbs or chewing His fingernails. He does not worry and, as His children, neither should we. God knows what He's doing. He has the whole world under control, and He has you and your loved ones in the palms of His hands.

CHAPTER THREE
The Heavy Handbag of Hopelessness and Discouragement

"O LORD, thou hast deceived me, and I was deceived: thou art stronger than I, and hast prevailed: I am in derision daily, every one mocketh me."
(Jeremiah 20:7)

There is a legend in which the devil had a yard sale of his tools—hatred, envy, jealousy, deceit, pride, and lying—and they were spread out on various tables. One tool in particular was set aside with an astronomical price tag, even though it was worn out more than any other tool. A customer asked, "What is this tool? Why is it so expensive?" The devil replied, "This tool is called discouragement, and it is so expensive because it is one of the most valuable tools I have. With it, I can pry open the hearts of individuals and get them so discouraged that they will not even try to use their faith and will be completely unwilling to trust God. I can use it to keep them from trying to do anything significant with their lives. That's why this tool has such a high price tag."

The astronomical price tag in that story must have kept the tool from selling because the devil still uses it every day. Discouragement is part of life, and it does not discriminate. There aren't many people who have not faced it at one time or another. Discouragement comes most often when we do the right thing but get poor results. Most likely, you know how that is. Perhaps you work eighty-hour weeks, but your business still fails. You spend all your time and resources on your children, but they rebel and live like prodigals. You practice and play hard but lose the game anyway. You do all the extracurricular activities, make honor roll, and volunteer service hours but don't get accepted to your school of choice. You eat right and exercise but can't seem to lose the weight

63

you want to lose.

Discouragement can eat a hole in your heart and leave a sense of void. It makes us want to ask, "Why even try?" It makes us want to quit. We can find ourselves so spiritually discouraged that we wave our fists at God and tell Him how upset we are that He didn't give us better results. That's exactly what Jeremiah did. God called Jeremiah to speak a harsh message to the rebellious people of Judah, and so he did. Yet, even in the midst of his obedience, Jeremiah found himself discouraged because of unfavorable results.

> WE CAN FIND OURSELVES SO SPIRITUALLY DISCOURAGED THAT WE WAVE OUR FISTS AT GOD AND TELL HIM HOW UPSET WE ARE THAT HE DIDN'T GIVE US BETTER RESULTS.

In Jeremiah 20, it turned out that Jeremiah's preaching had angered a man named Pashur, who was one of the assistants to the high priest and was also the chief security officer in the Temple. Pashur got so angry with Jeremiah and his message that he grabbed Jeremiah, beat him, and threw him into prison. Pashur locked Jeremiah in stocks so that his body was immobile. Jeremiah couldn't lie down, rest, or get comfortable in his prison cell. If he tried to sleep, his body weight would pull against the stocks and cause him pain. So Jeremiah, after having been obedient—*not* disobedient—to God, suffered this horrible persecution.

His situation shows that you can do right and still have difficult experiences in life. Jeremiah was locked up in prison and dealt with physical, emotional, and spiritual anguish. He had obeyed God but was beaten and locked up anyway. He became burdened with the heavy handbag of hopelessness and discouragement. Fortunately, Jeremiah found four handles on this handbag to lift it off and rebound from his situation. Let's take a look at the four handles that helped Jeremiah and can also help us get out from underneath the heavy handbag of hopelessness and discouragement.

PRESENT THE PAIN

The first handle to help us lift this bag is to present the pain in our lives to God. In Jeremiah 20:7-8, Jeremiah went to God in prayer and said what he was feeling: "O LORD, thou hast deceived me, and I was deceived; thou art stronger than I, and hast prevailed: I am in derision daily, every one mocketh me. For since I spake, I cried out, I cried violence and spoil; because the word of the LORD was made a reproach unto me, and a derision, daily."

Observe how Jeremiah talked to God: He prayed honestly, transparently, and vulnerably. He even said he felt God had persuaded (deceived or enticed) him into ministry. Jeremiah obviously felt that since he had been called into the ministry, everything was supposed to be delightful and copasetic. Jeremiah's discouragement is the result of him prefabricating a set of assumptions about his life and his ministry that God never sanctioned. Discouragement, as Jeremiah discovered, is often the by-product of unfulfilled expectations that he had. In that we created the assumptions and expectations we tend to hold God liable in making those views come true, and when He doesn't, we feel He has deceived us.

Jeremiah came to discover what many of us in ministry also discover: In *ministry*, there is also *misery*. Beyond ministry, life in general can cause us to become discouraged; but because his expectations had not been met, Jeremiah was upset with God. We understand this, don't we? We've often heard it said to people who aren't living right or who may be experiencing some issues in their lives that they need to "get right with God." However, Jeremiah's story teaches us that you can be right with God and still have problems. Jesus said, "In the world you will have tribulation; but be of good cheer, I have overcome the world" (John 16:33, NKJV).

Jeremiah understood that God is not small. He went to God in honest prayer. "God, I can't handle it. I'm bringing my pain to You and telling You exactly how I feel. I feel like You deceived me and let me down. Look at me in these chains. You didn't warn this would happen!" Jeremiah was so honest, in fact, that you may have trouble reading what he said. Jeremiah teaches us that God can handle our questions. After all, He is God. When Jeremiah couldn't make sense of his life and the struggles he had to endure, when he couldn't handle it, when he couldn't bear the burdens anymore, he knew he could take them to God and He could and would handle them. When life gets crazy, as it sometimes does, God is more than able and competent to handle life for us.

Has there ever been a time in your life where life appeared to be unmanageable and unbearable? Has there ever been a time when you had more questions than you had answers? In these moments, you must learn to take your pains to God in prayer. If you want to get a handle on the heavy handbag of hopelessness and discouragement, you first must hold loosely to the things you assume or expect and go to God in prayer. When your expectations are not congruent with your reality, God says to bring your pains to Him.

PERSEVERE IN GOD'S PLAN

If you want to get a second handle on discouragement, there's something to learn from Jeremiah 20:9. Jeremiah was at the point of giving up. He had decided to quit preaching because it had caused him so much trouble and had made him the center of jokes around town. In fact, Jeremiah had determined he would not speak God's name at all. He had resolved to resign and decided he was turning in his resignation without the proper protocol of a two-week notice. His resignation was effective immediately!

Have you ever felt like you were through, like you've taken all you could take? Jeremiah's job was to preach. As a prophet to Judah, the southern part of the nation of Israel, his job was to challenge the people of Judah and also the king himself. Remember in the first chapter we looked at the life of the prophet Elijah and the depression he endured when he had to face King Ahab and the threats of Ahab's wife, Jezebel? Prophets had to be bold, fearless, confident, and unconcerned with the opinions of others. Prophets, after all, spoke for God.

This was Jeremiah's job, but he was so tired of being laughed at that he said he was done. He was finished! Kaput! Jeremiah said, "I

Quit! No more!" He couldn't take it, and his cup of grief had overflowed. In other words, Jeremiah had reached the existential breaking point, that moment in life where mentally, emotionally, psychologically, and, yes, even spiritually, you feel you are about to have a meltdown.

But (which is a word directly from Jeremiah 20:9) Jeremiah said that once he got home, took off his preaching cloak, kicked up his feet in front of the fire, and tried to relax, something happened. He couldn't sit still. He wasn't happy like he thought he would be in retirement. He may have felt like he was finished with God, but God wasn't finished with him. Suddenly, it became harder for Jeremiah to *keep* from preaching than it was for him to preach and deal with the haters. Jeremiah was not content to quit. He had to do what we also must learn to do when we find ourselves feeling discouraged: persevere. The second handle to help you move the heavy handbag of hopelessness and discouragement, as discovered in Jeremiah's life, is to persevere in God's plan for your life.

Look at how Jeremiah described his experience: "But his word was in mine heart as a burning fire shut up in my bones, and I was weary with forbearing, and I could not stay" (verse 9). When Jeremiah tried to give up, he found doing so impossible because he understood and appreciated God's plan and calling for his life. God had given him the gift of preaching and the desire to preach. His purpose and passion was like cosmic combustion in his heart. What strengthened, inflamed, and gave Jeremiah the passion to persevere amid his pains was the internalized Word of God that was shut up within his heart.

Internalizing God's Word was one of the significant keys in Jeremiah persevering. Allow me to outline briefly a plan of action for internalizing God's Word in your heart, for without His Word being persistently in you, you will soon faint and become weary in life.

Steps to internalizing God's Word:

1. Hear God's Word with the intent to obey it (Luke 11:28;

Revelation 1:3; 2:7, 11, 17, 28; 3:6, 13, 22; Deuteronomy 6:4; James 1:19).

2. Make time to read God's Word daily to know its overall content. Find or develop a Bible reading program or plan; and meditate on one phrase, verse, or word throughout the day.

3. Study God's Word to know the depths of its meaning.

4. Memorize God's Word in order to have fuel for meditation and for use in your ministry.

5. Meditate on God's Word for deeper understanding of the Word and food for your soul.

6. Apply the truth of God's Word to your life to show its value and reap its benefits.

7. Be motivated in knowing that internalizing the Word is the one and only secret God gives for success in our spiritual lives (Joshua 1:8; Psalm 1:1-3; James 1:25).

Coupled with the internalized Word of God, Jeremiah's capacity to persevere was due to him recognizing God's plan and purpose for his life. It was God who had called Jeremiah from his mother's womb and had commissioned him as a voice to the nations according to Jeremiah 1. Yet, Jeremiah still wanted to walk completely away from God's assignment for his life. We all have stood in Jeremiah's shoes as we have also contemplated quitting and walking away from God's assignment due to unfulfilled dreams.

Most times in life, it is not easy to actualize your goals and dreams. If you think in terms of sports, you're like an athlete trying to score. If it were easy to do, no one would be interested in watching. If it were easy, no one would pay you to do it. What makes an athlete worth the salary is the ability to score against opposition and opponents. As with Jeremiah, sometimes the crowd jeers or calls you names or laughs at your mistakes. What if your favorite athlete walked off the field or the court when someone booed or called him a name? He wouldn't do that. If he (or she) did, that person wouldn't be your favorite athlete. What you want to see is the athlete score in the face of jeering, laughter, and boos. You want to see him keep focus, bounce back off the ropes, leap up from the canvas, and win the bout.

Remember how they booed Venus Williams when she first played at Wimbledon? They wondered what she was doing there— a girl from Compton! They criticized her looks. They doubted her ability to play against tennis greats at the All England Club in London, England, on an international platform. She faced opposition and was only sixteen years old. You can bet everyone knows who she is now. Five Wimbledon championships later, she is definitely well known as one of the most dominant players in the history of the sport. The records display her name and her sister Serena's name more than any other women in the history of the sport, and no opponent is more feared or respected on the other side of the net. That's what you want from your favorite athlete.

And that's what God wants from you.

When God gives you a gift and a goal and shows you His plan, you will come against opposition like any athlete on any field of competition. You will have to face the opposition and push past it. Sure, it gets hard. You'll want to quit at times, no doubt; but if you keep focused on God's plan for your life, you'll find a new fire inside you that will help you get through it.

Imagine having a child with a gift and a desire to sing, and you tell her the only song she should sing is "So Low and Far Away." Isn't that a mean thing to say to a child? That's what they said to Grammy nominee Chanté Moore, but she kept singing anyway.

Perhaps you have a dream to do something no one your age has ever done before, but everyone laughs in your face. George Foreman understands. George had aged and gotten out of shape. People thought he was crazy because he named all five of his sons after himself. For many, he was just the guy hocking grills on infomercials late at night. People forgot he was once the world heavyweight champion and Olympic gold medalist.

When, at the age of forty-five, George said he thought he could be the world heavyweight champion again by fighting a man twenty years younger, people thought he was really crazy—until he won! And those grills that some thought were foolish netted Forman over two hundred million dollars, which is far more than he ever made as a boxer. Certainly, George would tell you to keep on pursuing the ideas, desires, and goals you have.

When God gives you a plan, persevere. What if Jeremiah had quit? What if he hadn't persevered in God's plan for his life? Do you think we would be talking about his life today, three thousand years after he died? I don't think so. You don't achieve that kind of longevity and historical worth by quitting. You achieve that kind of impact by persevering. That, by the way, is why the devil is so interested in discouraging you. He doesn't want God's plan for your life to bear fruit. He wants you to die on the vine, give up, quit, and throw in the towel. If, however, you know God has a plan for your life, that fire inside you can ignite when you want to quit, giving you a new power to go forward. Oddly enough, Jeremiah didn't see how the word that exited his mouth had any effect on his surroundings and didn't realize it was working on him on the inside.

Whatever you do, don't quit. Persevere. The great poet Edgar A. Guest offers these inspiring words in his poem "See It Through":

> When you're up against a trouble,
> Meet it squarely, face to face;
> Lift your chin and set your shoulders,
> Plant your feet and take a brace.
> When it's vain to try and dodge it,
> Do the best that you can do;
> You may fail, but you may conquer,
> See it through!
> Black may be the clouds about you
> And your future may seem grim,
> But don't let your nerve desert you;
> Keep yourself in fighting trim.
> If the worst is bound to happen,

Spite of all that you can do,
Running from it will not save you,
See it through!
Even hope may seem but futile,
When with troubles you're beset,
But remember you are facing
Just what other men have met.
You may fail, but fall still fighting;
Don't give up, whate'er you do;
Eyes front, head high to the finish
See it through![5]

How hard can it get along the way? *Very.* And discouraging. In fact, Jeremiah never had a single convert in all his time preaching. He was called to preach and had a fire in his bones, but he wasn't the Venus Williams of the prophet world. That honor went to Elijah, the one who suffered from depression. Jeremiah wasn't well known for his great sermons. He never called down fire from heaven or traveled in whirlwinds as Elijah had. God did not give him that gift. Jeremiah was known only for being the laughing stock of Judah and dubbed as the "weeping prophet." He didn't have followers who came and comforted him after he was taunted by the people. He didn't have a corner man to pour water over his head after a round of brutal fighting. He didn't have any evidence to show he was indeed called except for the passion and fire he had in his heart, his own understanding of his calling and purpose in God.

PERCEIVE GOD'S PRESENCE

Sometimes when you are doing what God wants you to do, it can feel like a lonely journey. That sense of loneliness can make it harder to get a grip on the heavy handbag of hopelessness and discouragement. However, in Jeremiah 20:11, we find a third handle: "But the LORD is with me as a mighty terrible one: therefore my persecutors shall stumble, and they shall not prevail: they shall be greatly ashamed; for they shall not prosper: their everlasting confusion shall never be forgotten." The handle we find in this verse helps when you feel like you're all alone or that no one is in your corner. When you start to feel alone, do what Jeremiah did: perceive God's presence in your life.

The American Indians had a unique practice of training young braves. On the night of a boy's thirteenth birthday, after learning hunting, scouting, fishing, and various other skills, he was put to one final test. He was placed in a dense forest to spend the entire night alone. Until then, he had never been away from the security of his tribe miles away. When he took off the blindfold, he was terrified! Every time a twig snapped, he visualized a wild animal ready to pounce. After what seemed like an eternity, dawn broke and the first rays of sunlight entered the interior of the forest. Looking around, the boy saw flowers, trees, and the outline of the path. Then, surprised, he saw a man standing a few feet away, armed with a bow and arrow. It was his father. He had been there all night long, ready to protect and defend his son.

Just like our heavenly Father.

We must perceive His presence in our lives. That's the handle Jeremiah gives us in verse 11. You may feel like you're trying to lift this heavy handbag by yourself and that no one understands or cares. No one is in your corner; no one has your back. Jeremiah reminds us that none of these perceptions we have of being alone are real. God is always with us, so we need not worry about our adversities or our adversaries. We don't need to worry about what other people think or say. We don't need to worry about those who stand against us because, as Paul says in Romans 8:31, "If God be for us, who can be against us?" That doesn't mean no one can oppose you; it only means no one can overcome you.

In Jeremiah 20:12, Jeremiah reminds us that God does not travel alone: "But, O LORD of hosts." *Host* means army. Not only is God with us, but all His angelical army is with us as well. The psalmist speaks of how they are encompassed all about us. God, at any moment, can dispatch a legion of angelical emissaries to defend and deliver us. As a matter of fact, the writer of Hebrews defines them as "ministering spirits." God travels with backup so that you are not alone. Often in our discouragement, we look inward—to our problems, frustrations, and situations—when we should look upward to our God who has not abandoned us. He is with us. He accompanies us. He is a very present help in trouble.

Can you imagine the difference it would make in your outlook if you remained consciously aware that God is with you? Imagine going into a difficult board meeting knowing God is beside you. Picture entering into a stressful presentation knowing God walks with you. Envision confronting the status quo with the mighty arm of the Lord surrounding you.

Knowledge of God's presence can help us accomplish significant things despite our discouragement. Knowing God is with us provides courage, valor, strength, tenacity, and perseverance. Living in the glow of God's presence enables us to fight and press on despite discouragement.

So many times we throw pity parties over who walked out on us, used us, or abused us. Undoubtedly, we feel pain when someone leaves us; however, we must look up instead of around to recognize that it's not about who left us but who is still with us. Hebrews 13:5 reminds us that God has promised us, as believers, that He will never leave us nor forsake us. This is a one-way promise that is not dependent on our actions. It is God's promise. He won't leave us.

Some people are tempted to interpret this verse to mean that God won't leave us, but the truth is that we can walk away from God. Jeremiah tried to leave God, but God wouldn't let him. If we walk away from God, as Jeremiah tried to do, guess what? God goes where we go because He promised never to leave us. Wherever you are, God is with you. However, discouragement can cause you to *feel* distant from God and abandoned by Him.

If you ever think you've messed up too much and have gone too far, it's not so. If you ever think God has turned His back on you, it's not so. If you ever find yourself in a place that feels like

God is not there, it's not so. He is wherever you are, whenever you're there.

PROCLAIM GOD'S PRAISE

By Jeremiah 20:13, the prophet broke out in praise. All of his complaining turned to singing: "Sing unto the LORD, praise ye the LORD: for he hath delivered the soul of the poor from the hand of evildoers." Therefore, the fourth and final handle to help us get hold of the heavy handbag of hopelessness and discouragement and toss it away is to proclaim God's praise in your life.

Praise is the one weapon in the Christian's arsenal for which Satan has no defense. When we praise God, we acknowledge that He is in charge—He can do what He wants, when He wants, and how He wants. Praise is more than acknowledging God for the good that comes our way. Praise is accepting from God *all* that comes our way, both the good and the bad. The praise we offer when things don't go our way is far more precious to God than the praise we offer when all is well. As a matter of fact, God takes personal interest in our praise to Him. Psalm 22:3 says that God inhabits the praise of His people.

Let me help you develop a framework for your praise. There are four things praise will accomplish in our lives. First, when we praise God, it helps redirect our focus. Praise takes our minds off our situation and focuses us on God. As we praise God, we are essentially magnifying God. To *magnify* means "to make bigger, larger, to amplify." In other words, our praise supersizes our God and miniaturizes our problems. It gives God the right to rule and to reign in our lives however He sees fit. Praise redirects our focus by enabling us to acknowledge that God knows more about what He is doing than we do. It accepts that God can take all the bad stuff of life and make something beautiful out of it.

Second, praise will rekindle our faith. In Jeremiah 29:11, the prophet records God's words to Israel: "For I know the plans I have for you . . . plans for your welfare, not for disaster, to give you a future and a hope" (HCSB). Although this verse is spoken to the nation of Judah, it is appropriate for Jeremiah and for us as well. God weaves a tapestry out of our lives. We don't always see the finished product. We may not fully understand how He's going to accomplish His plans, but when we praise God, no matter where we are in the journey, we are saying to God that we trust He has it under control; and the more we practice our faith, the stronger our faith gets. As we continue to see how God keep His promises, our trust grows.

Third, praise will relieve our frustration because it is difficult for us to have a negative attitude when we are praising God. Nike has used its slogan since the 1980's: "Just do it!" You've likely heard that slogan hundreds of times. Have you ever had something to do and not wanted to do it? Did you ever then say to yourself, "Just do it"? Just do what you have to do. Then, when you start to do it, suddenly the thing you've been dreading gets easier. Sometimes it turns out to be downright simple—so simple you may even have trouble figuring out why you took so long to begin it in the first place.

That's how I feel with writing this book. I've wanted to write a book for a long time, but I kept procrastinating. Every time I go out to speak, people ask me if I have a book. People have said I should write a book. Well, I put it off long enough. I decided to just do it, and since I made that decision, it's become so much easier than I imagined.

Indecision breeds frustration. When you're frustrated and discouraged, you're waffling between trust and doubt; but when you praise God, you are throwing doubt out the window and going all out with trust. Your current situation may have you wondering what should you praise God for. It doesn't matter. Praise Him for anything and everything! When you start to praise God, you will see your spirit lift because God inhabits the praise of His people.

Fourth, praise releases God's favor. Your act of praise is itself an act of faith. Discouragement does not get along well with faith. You might even say that every time faith shows up, discouragement runs out the back door. Faith also does not get along well with

75

> THE POWER OF THE GOD WHO CREATED THIS UNIVERSE IS WITHIN OUR REACH WHEN WE PRAISE HIM.

frustration. Frustration is based on a sense of being overwhelmed, confused, and weak. Faith, on the other hand, is based on certainty, power, and confidence.

When you praise, you exercise faith. Psalm 34:8 says, "O taste and see that the LORD is good: blessed is the man that trusteth in him." This verse says you are blessed just by trusting God. But how do you trust? By exercising faith. If you want to see what God will do, exercise faith in Him by praising Him. Taste and see. Do it right now as you read this. Give God some praise, and see how it makes you feel. Taste and see that He is good. Be blessed by trusting Him. Isn't it amazing?

The power of the God who created this universe is within our reach when we praise Him. He can turn our sorrows into joy and our dark nights into days. He can deliver us from discouragement.

> THROUGH GOD'S POWER, WE CAN GRAB HOLD OF THE FOUR HANDLES ON THIS HANDBAG OF HOPELESSNESS AND DISCOURAGEMENT AND HURL IT RIGHT INTO HIS ARMS.

He can take away our heaviness and place on us the garment of praise. Through God's power, we can grab hold of the four handles on this handbag of hopelessness and discouragement and hurl it right into His arms. Present to God your pain, persevere in God's plan, perceive God's presence, and proclaim God's praise. When you do, watch God remove the hopelessness and discouragement from your life and make your journey lighter, smoother, and happier.

Let me encourage you to declare by faith the following victory pledge over discouragement:

I'm too anointed to be disappointed,
Too blessed to be depressed or distressed,
Too chosen to be frozen,
Too elected to be rejected,
Too inspired to be tired.
I have more to shout about than to pout about and
more to sing about than complain about!
I choose not to be discouraged!

CHAPTER FOUR
The Grievous Grip of Guilt

"For God so loved the world that he gave his only begotten Son, that whosoever believeth in him should not perish, but have everlasting life. For God sent not his Son into the world to condemn the world; but that the world through him might be saved."
(John 3:16-17)

As you've likely noticed throughout this book, I've done my best to come up with alliterative names for these bags to help you remember them. I had to go way back for this one. Decades ago, if you had a personal bag that you kept with you everywhere you went, one you wouldn't check with the porter on a train or with the skycap at the airport, one that carried your most personal items—the things you wanted to keep within your reach at all times—that bag was not known as a carry-on, as it is nowadays; it was called a grip.

If you happen to be one of my old-school readers, you might remember a song that came out in the disco era by the group Heatwave. The song was called "Groove Line," and it talked about the bag I want to discuss in this chapter. The lyric to the song said, "Pack your grip, taking you on a trip."

> GUILT IS OFTEN PERSONAL, PRIVATE, AND OFTEN LINKED TO OUR PASTS, TO THINGS WE KEEP CLOSE TO US.

The fact that the bag is called a grip and is used to store your most intimate and personal items is fitting. Guilt is often personal, private, and often linked to our pasts, to things we keep close to us. It is also something that can easily be described as having a tremendous grip on us. We all have experienced guilt in our lives because we are all sinners. Guilt is the by-product of sin. Another way to say it is, "If sin is the root, guilt is the fruit." Thus, where there is sin, there is guilt. We are guilty people by nature—guilty of impure thoughts, false statements, and harmful and hurtful deeds and words. All of us are guilty before a holy and righteous God. Because we have all sinned, we all stand in need of forgiveness and God's grace.

The wonderful thing is, although we are sinners, God has provided forgiveness for our sins through the death, burial, and resurrection of His Son. Because Jesus paid for our sins on the cross of Calvary, we no longer need to carry the grievous grip of guilt in our lives. Still, many of us seem burdened with this bag. For some of us, it seems the more guilt we have, the closer we feel to God. That is not what God wants, however.

Jesus has paid the price; He doesn't need you trying to pay the price again. You need to unpack that guilt and leave it behind for the rest of your trip. In Psalm 32, we can take a look at David, a prolific songwriter, who learned how to do just that.

THE GREATEST SONGWRITER IN HISTORY

Coincidentally, the previously mentioned group Heatwave had one of the most prolific songwriters in the history of music in America as its keyboardist—Rod Temperton. You may not recognize Rod Temperton's name, but you will definitely recognize the songs he wrote for some of the greatest artists of all time. For Heatwave, he wrote "Always and Forever"—that great love song they play on the oldies stations during the "Quiet Storm." In fact, he wrote all of their songs, including their most successful: "Boogie Nights" and "Groove Line." For the group The Brothers Johnson, he wrote "Stomp" and "Light Up the Night." For George Benson, he wrote "Give Me the Night." For Anita Baker, he wrote "Mystery." For James Ingram and Patty Austin, he wrote "Baby, Come to Me." For James Ingram and Michael McDonald, he wrote "Ya Mo Be There." And most famously, for Michael Jackson, he wrote "Rock with You"; "Off the Wall"; "Burn This Disco Out"; "Baby Be Mine"; and the title track to the biggest selling album in history,

"Thriller."

The amazing thing is that Temperton originally offered every one of the songs he is most famous for to Heatwave to record, but they rejected them. Temperton first offered all these songs to Heatwave because if Johnny Wilder Jr., Heatwave's lead singer and band leader, hadn't posted the ad in a magazine for a keyboardist that Rod answered, you may have never heard any of these songs.

Long before there was a Rod Temperton, however, there was David. There are 150 psalms in the Bible, and David wrote more than half of them. In the three thousand years since David's death, millions of songs in thousands of languages have been written either directly from or based on his psalms. David is, undoubtedly, the greatest songwriter in history. Like all songwriters, David wrote songs about experiences he'd had in his life—the good, the bad, and the ugly. That's what we find in Psalm 32, a psalm of David's penitence.

The Bible tells us that David was a man after God's own heart. In fact, 1 Kings 15:5 tells us "David did that which was right in the eyes of the LORD, and turned not aside from any thing that he commanded him all the days of his life, save only in the matter of Uriah the Hittite." That's quite a testimony. David was a righteous man until he made one major mistake.

To summarize 2 Samuel 11, David sent his men out to war and stayed behind in the comfort of the palace, even though it was the time of year when kings went to war. One night, he went for a stroll on the roof of the palace and looked down to notice a beautiful woman, Bathsheba, bathing. He learned she was the wife of Uriah, one of his faithful soldiers, but he didn't care. He sent for her, slept with her, and got her pregnant.

Then David had his general, Joab, send Uriah home. David hoped Uriah would sleep with Bathsheba and cover things up, but Uriah was so faithful to his duty as a soldier, he wouldn't do it. Unlike David, he refused to enjoy himself while his fellow countrymen were being killed fighting a war. So David invited him to a feast, got him drunk, and tried to send him home again, but Uriah didn't go. David then decided to send Uriah to the front line and ordered Joab to put him at the fiercest front and then withdraw from him so he would be killed. Along with Uriah, a number of David's other soldiers were killed as part of this cover-up. David then moved Bathsheba into the palace to become his wife, and she had his son.

David figured he'd gotten away, but God had a twist for this plot. He sent the prophet Nathan to tell David a story. Nathan told David about a rich man who had thousands of sheep and cattle and a poor man who had only one. The poor man's sheep grew up with his family like a pet from the time it was a little ewe; he even slept with it in his arms. Nathan then said that a traveler came to visit the rich man. Instead of taking one of his many sheep or cattle, he took the poor man's sheep and killed it to serve the traveler for dinner. Can you imagine Nathan telling David this story over a cup of tea? David got furious and self-righteous and said the man was wicked, that he must die! He must pay four times over for being so merciless. That's when Nathan dropped the bomb: "You are that man!"

God had seen the entire thing. Nathan told David that he may have gotten Bathsheba, but God said he would take all of David's wives and give them to someone close to him who would sleep with them in broad daylight. What a payback! David had done his sin in secret, but God was going to expose His judgment publically. In addition, Nathan said that God would spare David's life in exchange for his son's.

I can imagine David was immediately racked with guilt. Because of his lack of self-control, a number of his most faithful soldiers were dead. Children were fatherless. Wives were widowed. Homes were broken. His love child was taken away. An entire life of service, discipline, and righteousness was washed away. God knew. Nathan knew. Joab knew. His actions would be recorded in the annals of history—everybody would know.

Years later, David's other son Absalom tried to take over the throne in an act of insurrection and rebellion. To show that he was the new king, he slept with all of David's wives on the roof of the palace, just as God had said. So David was reminded of his sin for many years.

Out of this experience came so many of the psalms we read today for inspiration and encouragement in our times of struggle, including Psalm 32. In fact, Psalms 51 and 32 are companion psalms about this incident. Psalm 51 records David's confession of sin and his prayer for forgiveness. Psalm 32 expresses David's feelings prior to and following his forgiveness and restoration.

Though guilty, David found forgiveness from God for his sin. In Psalm 32, David looks in the rearview mirror at the most shameful moment of his life and invites believers to learn from his mistakes. Looking at this psalm by David, we can learn how to get rid of guilt's grievous grip.

THE PAIN OF SIN

By juxtaposing David's statements in Psalms 32 and 51, we can learn a lot about the guilt David felt before his forgiveness. There are four lessons in Psalm 32 that illuminate the nature of guilt.

First, we see the perversion or pain we feel when we commit sin. Verses 1-2 read, "Blessed is he whose transgression is forgiven, whose sin is covered. Blessed is the man unto whom the LORD imputeth not iniquity, and in whose spirit there is no guile." The word *blessed* means "happy." When we compare this declaration with what he writes in Psalm 51, it's easy to see David's former state under the grip of guilt. Psalm 51:1-3 says, "Have mercy upon me, O God, according to thy loving kindness: according unto the multitude of thy tender mercies blot out my transgressions. Wash me thoroughly from mine iniquity, and cleanse me from my sin. For I acknowledge my transgressions: and my sin is ever before me."

Notice how these two psalms fit together. David didn't feel blessed in Psalm 51. In fact, he felt miserable. Guilt haunted him. He felt dirty, evil, broken, guilty, and as though his sin was always on his mind. His guilt was so grievous that David uses four different Hebrew words to describe the sin that produces it.

The first word, *sin*, means "defect or falling short of what is required." You know how you take the driving test to get your license and you either pass or fail? That's a good way to view the word *sin*. Sin is simple: You failed the test. You did not complete what you were required to do. You missed the mark of approval. It does not matter if you were close to passing. It does not matter if you had good intentions or a good reason for not passing or if you passed every other practice test you took. Sin means you have failed.

The second word is *transgression*. This word means "defiance or rebellion against authority." If you're like me, you may be reminded of this one most with your kids. You tell a child to do one thing, and he does exactly the opposite from what you say. We, too, are like that with God, in both active and passive ways. God tells us to love our enemies and not to do harm, but we're often too busy planning our revenge.

In David's case, the transgression came in his disobedience to God's command not to commit adultery and not to covet his neighbor's wife. It's in the Ten Commandments (Exodus 20:14, 17). David knew this. He knew what he was doing was wrong, but he did not care. In a real sense, David had trespassed. He went beyond the prescribed lines that were established by God.

The third word is *iniquity*, which means "to pervert that which is good or moral wickedness." Iniquity is a distortion or perversion of good. Jesus said that it was better that a millstone be tied around your neck and cast into the sea than that you cause a child to fall into sin (Matthew 18:6). A child is innocent and pure, and causing a child to sin is iniquity.

In David's case, he damaged Bathsheba and Uriah's holy matrimony. He also destroyed the families of the men who died with Uriah—their children were fatherless and their wives widowed. Furthermore, since the husband provided for the family and women were not able to find work, those families were also likely impoverished; they were turned from self-supporting units into dependent beggars. David did all that so he could have Bathsheba.

83

David's life teaches us that our sins can have a radical and profound negative impact upon others.

The final word David uses is *guile*, which means "to project something false, to be cunning and crafty." David used guile when he tried to get Uriah to go home to have sex with his wife so David would be off the hook as the baby's father. That was sneaky, James Bond 007 kind of stuff. Guile is the lying, the twisting of the truth, the private numbers, the secret e-mail accounts, the hidden stash. Guile is the cover-up.

Ignoring or explaining away sin only intensifies it. David is telling us in these two psalms to let sin drive you to God, in whom you will find boundless mercy and amazing grace to restore your soul. In Psalm 51, David confessed and pleaded for God's mercy. In Psalm 32, he received the mercy he sought. It was his confession that led to forgiveness. First John 1:9 says, "If we confess our sins, he is faithful and just to forgive us our sins, and to cleanse us from all unrighteousness." As David used multiple words to describe different types of sin, he also used multiple words to describe the nature of God's forgiveness.

The first of these words is *forgiven*, which means "to take away the burden." Throughout this book, we've been discussing the idea of unpacking or laying aside heavy emotional baggage. We are seeking ways to have God relieve us of the weight of the excess stuff we carry around. In essence, we are seeking to live our lives in the full awareness that we are forgiven. This quality of life can only be experienced through Christ, of whom Scripture says, has come to take away the sins of the world (John 1:29).

The second word for forgiveness is *covered*, which means "to put out of sight." God puts our sins out of His sight. He will never bring up our sins as a matter of judgment between Him and us. When we are in Christ, His blood covers our sins. Psalm 103:12 says, "He has removed our sins as far from us as the east is from the west" (NLT). Micah 7:19 says, "You will again have compassion on us; you will tread our sins underfoot and hurl all our iniquities into the depths of the sea" (NIV). That's worth shouting over!

God can cover our sins. As stated in a sermon preached by Dr. Jeffrey Arthurs based on Psalm 32, we can either futilely attempt to cover our sins or allow God to cover them. The latter option is the obvious best choice.

The final word for forgiveness is *not imputed*, which means our sin debt is cancelled. Jesus pays the penalty of our sin. Such is the power and value of forgiveness: If we confess our sin, God's bookkeeping system bills Jesus for it, whose blood has already paid for our sins.

This wonderful forgiveness is available to us but only when we follow God's instructions for forgiveness through confession. Many of us never experience freedom from the grievous grip of guilt because we try to conceal our sins. The second lesson we can draw from Psalm 32:3-4 is the problem we face when we conceal sin.

THE PROBLEMS OF SIN

When David initially sinned, he kept silent. The poet Alexander Pope once said, "To err is human." Someone later added, "To cover it up is, too." When we sin, our tendency is not to confess but to conceal it. In verses 3-4, David said when he attempted to conceal his sin, the burden of his sin followed him everywhere he went. Here is a reliable principle: "If you don't deal with your guilt, your guilt will deal with you." We'll have no sense of joy and no sense of ease, because guilt creates a nagging sense of unrest and internal irritation within.

David said that the guilt he felt over his sin made him feel like he was missing the one thing he needed in his life. Where David once had vitality, guilt made him feel dried up. David said his "moisture is turned into the drought of summer" (Psalm 32:4).

Have you ever had dry mouth? Have you ever been thirsty and couldn't get enough to drink? Have you had dry skin? You put on lotion, but it seems to evaporate. Your skin cracks. Your lips crack. Water is the body's number one need. You can go weeks without food, but you will barely make it a few days without water; and I can promise you that during that period, you will think of nothing other than water and how to get it. That's like the grip of guilt. It's a bag we simply can't afford to carry around because it can have such a grip on us.

Life becomes uncomfortable because, as Charles Spurgeon once said, "God does not allow His children to sin successfully."[6] When you hide your sin, you experience a drought of the soul. Understand, however, that you cannot hide from God once you sin. Adam and Eve falsely assumed that they could, only to discover otherwise when God asked Adam, "Where art thou?" (Genesis 3:9).

Instead of hiding, we actually quench the source of our spiritual life within us, the Holy Spirit, who also grieves when we sin. Not confessing sin causes our spiritual functions to shut down as we wrestle with our consciences. Our love begins to flake and peel. Our kindness starts to recede, and our patience dries out.

In David's case, his sin was the wound, but his silence was the infection. God has made us to want fellowship with Him. He doesn't want anything to come between us. When we sin and fail to confess, we allow that sin to take precedent over our obligation to confess and be forgiven. The grip of guilt makes us know that something is not right, and it needs to be addressed quickly.

In Psalm 32:5, David finally explained what led to his declaration of being blessed: "I acknowledged my sin unto thee, and mine iniquity have I not hid. I said, I will confess my transgressions unto the LORD; and thou forgavest the iniquity of my sin." Here we see the pardon we find when we confess sin. David said that when he confessed his transgression, God "[forgave] the iniquity of [his] sin." By confessing, believers unlock God's grace through forgiveness.

Have you ever had people lie to you? Have you ever caught them in their own lies? You know they're lying, and they know they're lying, but they keep holding on to it. What makes it worse is that sometimes it's not even the thing they did that's a big deal; the bigger deal is that they think you're naïve enough to believe the lies. If they would confess, you'd let it go; but the fact that they won't admit what they've done makes forgiveness that much harder to give.

That's how it is when we sin against God. He already knows what we did, but we're so busy trying to cover it up that we think we are "pulling the wool over His eyes," so to speak. All He wants is the confession, so He can freely give us His grace.

David said in verse 5 that once he finally confessed and admitted all he'd done—staying behind during war, lusting for Bathsheba, committing adultery with a woman he knew was married and powerless to resist him, murdering Uriah and the other men who fell with Uriah, destroying innocent families—he found a degree of judgment but also found God's forgiveness, healing, restoration, joy, blessing, love, and grace.

God already knows what we've done. We are the ones carrying around the grievous grip of guilt. The starting point in turning our lives around when we have strayed is to be honest with the Lord Jesus about what we have done. If you are not willing to confess your sins and ask for God's forgiveness, you will never enjoy the deliverance God wants to give you. Confession is about admitting and agreeing with God that He is right and you are wrong. In order to find relief from this costly emotional baggage, we have to be ready, willing, and eager to confess our sins. When we confess, God is eager to forgive us. Proverbs 28:13 says, "People who conceal their sins will not prosper, but if they confess and turn from them, they will receive mercy" (NLT).

In Psalm 32:7, David went from hiding *from* God to hiding *in* God: "Thou art my hiding place; thou shalt preserve me from trouble; thou shalt compass me about with songs of deliverance." Doesn't hiding in God sound better than hiding from Him? David is talking about the pleasure we find when we confess our sin. Look at the joy he found. He learned about God's forgiveness and grew closer to Him. David stopped hiding from God and realized that God understood him better than he had ever believed.

I've noticed a sad tendency among some believers who think that the more guilt they feel, the closer they are to God. This is not true. In fact, nothing can be further from the truth. Jesus says in John 10:10, "The thief cometh not, but for to steal, and to kill, and to destroy: I am come that they might have life, and that they might have it more abundantly."

Jesus didn't come to make your life miserable and guilt-filled. Therefore, you are not closer to Jesus because you feel guilty and miserable. In fact, only the devil would want you to believe something like that. One of the ways the devil steals, kills, and destroys our joyful sense of fellowship with God is by injecting guilt, shame, and condemnation in our hearts. The devil will go to no ends in making us feel unaccepted, unloved, and unwanted by God.

People often memorize John 3:16, but they rarely acknowledge the next verse, John 3:17. We know the familiar passage, "For God so loved the world, that he gave his only begotten Son, that whosoever believeth in him should not perish, but have everlasting life." But look closely at the next verse: "For God sent not his Son into the world to condemn the world; but that the world through him might be saved." In this verse, Jesus clearly tells us that He is not interested in condemning us to eternal damnation or a sense of damnation in this life. He is not interested in our carrying around the grievous grip of guilt. If God wanted to condemn us, He would not have sent Jesus to save us. That's the miraculous message of the gospel.

If you have been carrying around guilt, Jesus wants you to stop. Put it down. Release your grip. Let it go. He died so that you would experience the pleasure of His pardon, the joy of His grace, the fullness of His love, and the life He's given you more abundantly.

By the way, it doesn't matter if you got this bag yourself or someone else gave it to you. Guilt can come in many forms—things you have done to others, things you were unable to do for others, things others said you should have done, things you could have controlled, and things you could not have controlled—but you must know that no matter how the grip of guilt came into your life, it can be removed by the blood of Jesus Christ.

Once you learn to confess your sin, you won't have to be controlled by the guilt it brings with it. Instead, you'll conquer the power of sin over your life. Experiencing God on this level led David to compose some of his greatest hits, which have been remixed for generations by people who learned to stop hiding from God and began to hide in God. Beneath the protective covering of His love and grace, you can find your way out from under the grievous grip of guilt and into the pleasure of God's pardon.

> BENEATH THE PROTECTIVE COVERING OF HIS LOVE AND GRACE, YOU CAN FIND YOUR WAY OUT FROM UNDER THE GRIEVOUS GRIP OF GUILT AND INTO THE PLEASURE OF GOD'S PARDON.

CHAPTER FIVE
The Problematic Pouch of People-Pleasing

"Fearing people is a dangerous trap, but trusting the LORD means safety."
(Proverbs 29:25 NLT)

Monique found a deal on a beautiful new summer dress. She had wanted a dress for a long time, and when she found one for only ten dollars, she was excited and bought it immediately. The first day she wore it, she asked her friend Sandra what she thought.

"It was on sale," Monique said, "Doesn't it look cute? It was the last one left."

Sandra looked her up and down, scrunched her nose, and said, "It's cute, but it kind of makes you look chubby."

Mortified, Monique ran home, took off the dress, and returned it to the store. Two days later, Monique ran into Sandra again, but this time Sandra was wearing the dress. "Hey, wait a minute. Where'd you get that? That looks exactly like the one I had."

"I know. That's because it is. Doesn't it look good on me?" Sandra replied.

Monique got upset but saw her chance to get even. "You know we're the same size. If it made me look fat, it makes you look fat, too."

Sandra shrugged her shoulders, "Perhaps. But I like it, and that's all that matters to me."

JUMPING THROUGH HOOPS

Early in my ministry, I realized how problematic it was for me to carry around the pouch of people-pleasing. It's natural for pastors to want to get along with people and please the church members; but I discovered that whenever I managed to please one person or group of people, I often upset and frustrated another. That's just the way people and organizations are. Furthermore, if trying to please people doesn't lead us to upsetting someone else, it can easily lead to us upsetting ourselves. Most people who spend their time trying to please people bend themselves through so many hoops that they sometimes don't even remember who they are anymore.

It is natural for people to want to please others. Employees want to please employers, students want to please teachers, spouses want to please each other, and children want to please their parents. But that's not really what I'm talking about in this chapter. I'm talking about people-pleasing that usually springs from low self-esteem.

Let me tell you what I mean so you can determine if you might be lugging around this bag. People-pleasing can be a sign of youth and inexperience. Children might change how they behave in order to be liked and look cool. Some "cool" boy cracks a joke about another kid's sneakers, and the kid goes home and begs his parents to get new sneakers so he can impress the "cool" boy next time. Of course we don't do that as adults, right? If we have this bag, maybe we do. Perhaps instead of it being a pair of sneakers, it's the car we drive, how we wear our hair, the clothes we wear, the people we hang out with, our career paths—you get the point. If you want to please people to the point of changing who you are, you might be carrying the problematic pouch of people-pleasing.

> IF YOU WANT TO PLEASE PEOPLE TO THE POINT OF CHANGING WHO YOU ARE, YOU MIGHT BE CARRYING THE PROBLEMATIC POUCH OF PEOPLE-PLEASING.

Some people-pleasers cannot take rejection or are so afraid of offending people that they allow people to walk all over them. Others do it because they are trying to get people to do something for them. However, there is a difference between those who occasionally go out of their way to do something in order to get a result from someone and those who live in fear that if they don't please others then they feel they have no value. For these latter people, this problematic pouch can become a giant sack that makes life miserable.

Comedian Jeff Foxworthy made a fortune off one catchphrase. He began thousands of jokes with "You might be a redneck if . . ." Because pleasing people can go either way, and there's a fine line between doing it in a healthy way and being hurt or burdened by it, I'm going to borrow his technique to help explain it better.

- If you can't say no because you're afraid of what someone might think or say, you might be a people-pleaser.
- If you are always smiling and never get angry with anyone, but instead bottle the anger inward and implode on yourself, you might be a people-pleaser.
- If you worry about what everyone thinks about you, you might be a people-pleaser.
- If the opinion of other people matters to you more than your own opinion, you might be a people-pleaser.
- If you sacrifice your happiness in order to win someone's approval, you might be a people-pleaser.
- If you are always apologizing for no particular reason, you might be a people-pleaser.
- If you are a sucker for flattery—someone gives you a compliment and you're ready to give him the keys to your house— you might be a people-pleaser.
- If you are terrified of confrontation and worried that someone will stop being your friend or won't like you, you might be a people-pleaser.
- If you go into debt buying gifts for people in hopes they will like you, you might be a people-pleaser.

Even Jesus couldn't please everyone. Matthew 21:15 says, "When the chief priests and scribes saw the wonderful things that he did, and the children crying in the temple and saying, Hosanna to the Son of David; they were sore displeased." He is both the perfect man and God Himself, so if Jesus can't please everyone, what makes us think we can? This little pouch, though helpful in some situations, can be horribly burdensome if it dominates our lives.

In this chapter, I want to take a look at how we can learn to find our validation and acceptance in God alone, not by worrying about other people's opinions of us. To rid ourselves of the problematic pouch of people-pleasing, we're going to need to take a look at some characters in the Bible who struggled with this problem and then how the apostle Paul learned to toss this bag out of his life.

THE TRAPS OF PEOPLE-PLEASING

Proverbs 29:25 says, "Fearing people is a dangerous trap, but trusting the LORD means safety" (NLT). This passage from Solomon, the person the Bible calls the wisest man to ever live, says that people-pleasing is a trap.

There are several ways in which being an approval addict, or a people-pleaser, is a trap. This first trap has to do with being more concerned about fulfilling whatever purpose some person has fabricated for us than we are about fulfilling God's purpose for our lives. The point is that being a people-pleaser blocks us from being a God pleaser; it compromises our purpose.

In 1 Thessalonians 2:4, Paul says, "But just as we have been approved by God to be entrusted with the gospel, so we speak, not as pleasing men, but God who examines our hearts" (NASB). Paul says that, as believers, we have already been approved by God. Once God approves us, who needs to second it? Absolutely nobody! At the end of the day, God is the judge of all mankind. So if He approves and is pleased, why are we worried about other people's opinions? The only thing that matters is whether we please God.

It really doesn't make sense, does it? It's like winning the lottery for millions of dollars and being upset that Visa turned you down for a credit card. Why do you need a credit card when you have millions of dollars? How can you be upset about a single opinion, or even lots of opinions, when you have all the approval you need for the rest of your life from God?

Still, that's the trap we fall into when we carry around the pouch of people-pleasing. We place more weight and credence on the approval of man than the approval of God who examines each of our hearts.

The second way in which being a people-pleaser is a trap is that it cripples our productivity. John 5:44 says, "How can you believe, when you receive glory from one another and you do not seek the glory that is from the one and only God?" (NASB). When we are people-pleasers, our growth and development as believers is short-circuited because we're more concerned with being praised by one another than we are with being praised by God.

You may have seen this principle at work in your family or perhaps among your friends when you were younger. Perhaps a teen who is so concerned with what his friends think that he doesn't care at all what his parents think, so he does all kinds of terrible things, sometimes even damaging his future and risking his own life because his friends do it or think he's cool for doing it. We hear about it on the news all the time. A carload of young teens crashes, resulting in fatalities or severe injuries, and alcohol or drugs are the culprits. Their parents told them not to, but they did it anyway to please their friends or to look "cool." We sometimes want approval from one another more than we want it from God. We want praise from our peers more than we want praise from God.

The third way in which people-pleasing is a trap is that it creates perversion in the form of peer pressure. Often we believe peer pressure is something that only occurs with children, but this is not true. Peer pressure does not discriminate. In fact, it can attack people of all ages, in both subtle and aggressive ways, with the purpose of making us conform to the wishes or demands of others in order to gain approval or acceptance. We never outgrow the pressure of our peers. If you carry the pouch of people-pleasing, you are particularly vulnerable to the perversion of peer pressure. In fact, the Bible speaks of several people who succumbed to this particular form of perversion.

After Jesus was arrested the night before His crucifixion, Peter was in the Temple court and was accused of being a friend of Jesus. Peter denied three times he even knew Jesus. On the third time, he was so desperate to be approved, he even cursed for emphasis. Peter gave in to peer pressure; he was perverted by his desire to please people and not blow his cover as a disciple of Jesus Christ.

Pilate, at the trial of Jesus, decided to save face with the crowd, even though he could not find any justifiable reason to put Jesus to death. Pilate had been entrusted with justice in this region, but he sacrificed an innocent man's life for the sake of peer pressure. Pilate should have been Jesus's hero. As the Roman governor of Judea serving under Emperor Tiberius, he should have had nothing to fear from that mob. He had the protection of the Roman army, the strongest army in the world; but instead of telling the people to be quiet and go home because Jesus was innocent, he gave in to the perversion of peer pressure and ordered Jesus to be tortured and killed and "washed his hands" of the matter (Matthew 27:4).

Joseph's eleven brothers gave in to peer pressure among themselves. Not a single one was willing to stand up to protect their baby brother after plotting to get rid of him. The Bible says that his oldest brother, Reuben, wanted to come back to get him and return him to his father, but instead Reuben said nothing when they sold him into slavery. He never went back and told his father what happened; he kept quiet and did nothing. He watched his father suffer under the belief that wild animals had killed his son. Reuben and the rest of Joseph's brothers were perverted by peer pressure.

Even kings give into peer pressure and the desire to please people. King Saul in the Old Testament confessed to God, "I've sinned. I've trampled roughshod over God's Word and your instructions. I cared more about pleasing the people. I let them tell me what to do" (1 Samuel 15:24-25, MSG). Moses said in Exodus 23:2, "Thou shalt not follow a multitude to do evil"; but that is exactly what happens when we carry about the pouch of people-pleasing. We conform and become perverted by peer pressure.

The fourth trap of people-pleasing is that it contradicts our priorities, which we see in Paul's writing in Galatians 1:10: "Obviously, I'm not trying to win the approval of people, but of God. If pleasing people were my goal, I would not be Christ's servant" (NLT). In this verse, Paul discusses his former life as a Pharisee and his current life as an apostle. In his former life, he strove to please men by reconciling various points of view on doctrine in order to make members of different factions happy. As an apostle of Christ, however, he was only concerned with what God thought. He no longer concerned himself with what people thought because he prioritized his responsibility to God.

Paul says you can either have it one way or the other: You can either please God or people, but you can't do both. Paul says, "Obviously, I'm not worried about pleasing people because, if I were, I wouldn't be a servant of God." In other words, it's never been popular to be a servant of God. Serving God, by its very nature, interferes with pleasing people because, most times, what God wants and what people want contradict. Paul makes God his priority and is no longer trying to be socially and politically correct.

God wants us to be a challenge to the status quo, not the keepers of it. Think about Jesus when He went into the Temple and overturned the tables of the moneychangers. He interfered with people's livelihoods. Moneychangers made their money by changing people's currency (and cheating them in the process). Jesus messed with the whole system the Jewish leaders set up. It wasn't a popular thing for Jesus to do.

Many times, that's the case for believers as well. When you challenge the status quo, you often step on feet along the way. *Status quo* means the state of affairs. It's the state of affairs because it benefits those in power. If you stand with Jesus, you're likely to find yourself ousted from clubs and without an invitation to the balls. If you're a people-pleaser, that simply won't do.

The fifth trap of being a people-pleaser is it causes pretentiousness. You find yourself wearing a mask to match those you want to please. You may own a church mask, a work mask, a club mask, a professional mask, a friend mask, and a fraternity or sorority mask. You put on an appearance based on whom you are with. Being a people-pleaser can make you fake, unauthentic, and insincere.

Jesus addressed this when He said in Luke 16:15, "You like to appear righteous in public, but God knows your hearts. What this world honors is detestable in the sight of God" (NLT). People-pleasers pretend to be what/who they don't intend to be. They are chameleons who adapt to wherever they are. They are professional stage players, hypocrites.

If you've ever watched professional basketball, you know that, on occasion, they clip a live microphone on one of the players or coaches to give the audience an opportunity to listen in on what's being said in the huddles, during the skirmishes, while they're hanging around the free throw line, or running the court. If you want to get a feel for whether you might be the type of person Jesus is talking about in this passage, imagine if you were mic'd up and didn't know it. What if people from church could hear how you talk at work or vice versa? What if your family could hear you wherever you went? If that would be a problem for you, you might have an issue with pretentiousness that comes from people-pleasing.

The final trap people-pleasers can expect to fall into is when their Christianity gets in the way of their people-pleasing and they find themselves being closet Christians. People-pleasing conceals our profession of faith.

We often hear the saying, "There are two things you don't talk about: religion and politics." That's interesting because Jesus said to go into all the world and preach the gospel to everyone (Mark 16:15). So what do you do if you're a people-pleaser? You're going to have to disobey one of these two rules. Which will it be? You're either going to obey Jesus and talk about Him, or you're going to conceal your profession and hope to be liked. People-pleasers choose the latter more often than not.

We see many examples of closet Christians in the Bible.

Once the Jewish leaders decided to kill Jesus, they looked for

Him during the Festival of Tabernacles in Judea. John 7:13 says that people murmured about the miracles they saw and heard what He did, but that "no one had the courage to speak favorably about Him in public, for they were afraid of getting in trouble with the Jewish leaders" (NLT).

It happened again in John 9:22. Jesus healed a man who was born blind, and his parents witnessed it; but when the Jewish leaders came and asked how it happened, the parents said, "We know this is our son and that he was born blind, but we don't know how he can see or who healed him. Ask him. He is old enough to speak for himself" (John 9:20-21, NLT). His parents were afraid of the Jewish leaders who had announced that anyone who said Jesus was the Messiah would be expelled from the synagogue. These parents believed Jesus was the Messiah, but they were worried about losing their social group at the synagogue. How much fear is that? How misplaced are their loyalties?

It doesn't stop there. It happened again in John 12:42-43 where John revealed, "Many people did believe in him, however, including some of the Jewish leaders. But they wouldn't admit it for fear that the Pharisees would expel them from the synagogue. For they loved human praise more than the praise of God."

Not much has changed since then. There are plenty of Christians today who, if you didn't see them in church, you'd have no idea they were Christians. Many justify their silence when it comes to Jesus by saying, "We can't talk about religion and politics." Except we don't have any problem talking about *Scandal* or other hit shows we see on TV. In fact, we'll happily talk about *Scandal*. We'll attend a party to talk about that show. We'll adjust our schedule so we don't miss it. We'll pop popcorn and pour a glass of wine so we can be like Olivia Pope while we're watching Olivia Pope be scandalous. We'll talk about *Scandal*, but we won't talk about the One who kept us out of a scandal.

JESUS DIDN'T PLEASE EVERYONE

So how do we get rid of this problematic pouch of people-pleasing? It starts with recognizing that even Jesus couldn't please everyone. Matthew 21:14-15 gives a remarkable example of this: "And the blind and the lame came to him in the temple; and he healed them. And when the chief priests and scribes saw the wonderful things that he did, and the children crying in the temple, and saying, Hosanna to the Son of David; they were sore displeased."

Can you imagine what that must have been like? God was in the flesh in the form of Jesus Christ, among people who professed to love God and commit their lives to His service, but He received no love. He did all the things the prophets said He would do—healed the blind, the deaf, and the lame; taught in the synagogue; and fed the hungry—but these men weren't rejoicing like the children were. The children had enough sense to recognize what was going on; but the adults, the priest, the "holy" men of God, the servants of the Lord missed it completely. They weren't only unhappy, they were "sore displeased." Another word would be *indignant*—ticked off, vehement, livid, apoplectic, fuming, irate, furious, seething, incensed, outraged, umbrageous, hopping mad!

Jesus went about His business, healing and blessing people and ticking off the church leaders at the same time. If Jesus couldn't please everyone, how can you? It's really quite simple: You can't. You can't please everyone. It's not possible. Some people can't be happy or satisfied unless they are the ones being blessed. That's why Jesus didn't try to please everyone and why you shouldn't either. If Jesus had given the Pharisees more gold and jewelry to wear or honored them or gave them praise or more power, perhaps they would have loved Him. Instead, He healed people without the Phraisees' help; without their approval; without their blessing; and against their will, authority, and traditions. He showed people that the true path to God had nothing to do with the Pharisees.

In fact, the Pharisees were blocking people from getting to God. Jesus was there to do His Father's will. If He pleased His Father, He couldn't please the people who were in the way of His Father. The Pharisees and leaders were in the way. If you're going to live for Jesus, some people are going to be in your way, but you should not spend a moment trying to please them.

NOT EVERYONE WILL LIKE YOU

The second way to overcome the problematic purse of people-pleasing is similar to the first: Free yourself from the unrealistic idea that everyone is going to like you. In the 2012 presidential election, President Obama received 52 percent of the vote. His opponent received 48 percent. When he was inaugurated as the first African American president, over one million people stood in the freezing Washington, DC, air all night long for the chance to attend the historical event. Millions more watched on TVs all over the world; but there were millions of others who couldn't change the channel fast enough.

One hundred and fifty-three years earlier, black people were still slaves in America. Only fifty years ago, we couldn't drink from fountains in many places. We couldn't use certain bathrooms. We lived under apartheid conditions all over the Southern United States. Now we have a black president. Who wouldn't cheer for that? That's a hero story, and people always cheer for underdog heroes, right? Our nation should be so proud, right? Nope, not everybody.

As with Jesus, one week the people yelled, "Hosanna," and the next week they yelled, "Crucify him!" That's how people are. It doesn't matter how many hoops you jump through, some people aren't going to like you. They'll find a reason not to like you. They don't like you because you're tall, because you're short, because you're pretty, because you have this, because you have that, because you don't have this or that—sometimes they don't even need a reason not to like you. They just don't like you. Accept the fact that, like Jesus, you can't please everyone.

The third way to help you stop being an approval addict—a people-pleaser—is to stop basing your fulfillment and acceptance on people's opinions. Your attitude should be one in which only three opinions really matter in your life:

1. Your opinion of God
2. God's opinion of you
3. Your opinion of yourself

No one else's opinion has final rule. Read what Jesus said about this in John 5:30: "I can do nothing on my own. I judge as God tells me. Therefore, my judgment is just, because I carry out the will of the one who sent me, not my own will" (NLT). Jesus was focused on doing God's will. He was happy with Himself because He was doing what God wanted Him to do. That's how we should be.

God is not fickle; He doesn't change. He's the same yesterday, today, and forever. So when you please Him today, you know that behavior is still pleasing to Him tomorrow. He's not going to change His mind on you. He says He loves you today—that's still going to be true tomorrow. He's not going to leave you hanging. He's not going to switch His allegiance. He's not going to get some new friends He likes better. You can be assured in this.

The fourth way to free ourselves from this pouch of people-pleasing is to recognize that ultimately God is the only one we must please. Remember the Scripture from Paul we looked at earlier, "Obviously, I'm not trying to win the approval of people, but of God. If pleasing people were my goal, I would not be Christ's servant" (Galatians 1:10, NLT). It is our duty as believers to please God. This is a matter of obedience. Our goal should be to please God and not to worry about pleasing man as a matter of obedience as well as a matter of peace of mind. You can kill two birds with one proverbial stone in this case. You can please God, and you can rid yourself of the burden of trying to please people.

The fifth guideline is similar to the fourth, but it packs a little more punch. We need to recognize that we must give an account to God. As believers, we understand that one day we will stand before God and show our work.

Do you remember having to take tests in school where you had

to "show your work"? Not all tests were like that. With scantrons—
—those little slips of computer paper where you fill in the bubbles
with a #2 pencil—if you didn't know the answer, you filled in ran-
dom bubbles. There are usually four or five bubbles, so you have
about a 20-25 percent chance of getting the answer right if you
guess.

I know someone who ran out of time on his PSAT and ran-
domly guessed on the last thirty questions, filling in all thirty bubbles in about fifteen seconds. A few months later, his guidance
counselor called him into the office and told him that NASA had
sent a letter to the school asking the student to design a project for
the Space Shuttle. It turned out he had the highest score on the
PSAT in the city. This guy, however, had no idea how to design a
project for the Space Shuttle because he only had guessed lucky! In
fact, he had dropped physics earlier that year because it was too
much work.

The point is, sometimes you get lucky and guess right, but that
doesn't work so well when you have to "show your work." When
the test requires that you show your work, there is space on the
paper for you to show the exact calculations you used to come to
the answer. When you have to show your work, you can't guess;
you have to know what you're doing. "Well, Lord, I was trying to
impress so-and-so, and that's why I didn't do what You said."
That's not what you want to show God.

The final guideline for getting rid of this pouch of people-
pleasing is one that too many people today don't understand. The
fact of the matter is that God shaped you to be uniquely you. In all
honesty, many of us have to simply stop allowing people to come
up with their descriptions, their profiles, and their lists of require-
ments for us to be accepted by them. On the contrary, we must
each get to the point where we recognize that God has shaped us
to be uniquely who we are, and if others can't take that, perhaps
they don't deserve to be with us.

This is how you twist this whole rejection thing you might be
feeling. It's not them rejecting you. If they have a problem with

you, if they can't accept someone as unique, special, valuable, wonderful, and fearfully made as you, then that's their loss. *They* missed out on being with you. What did Beyoncé say? "You must not know 'bout me." They don't know what you bring to the table. They don't know how to respect you. They don't understand how loved you are already. They don't get it. Poor them. You know who you are. You are a child of God. You know you are accepted and beloved. You know you are saved and approved. You know you are blessed. You know you are gifted, talented, and worthy.

KNOW YOU ARE A DIAMOND

Once an old prospector walked up to a young prospector outside a river in the Sierra Nevada Mountains of California during the gold rush. The young miner was sifting through some sludge knee-deep in the cold river. The old man said, "How's it going, young fella?"

The young miner said, "Not much today, pops."

The old man said, "Let's see yer pickins."

The young guy showed him a couple of tiny, shiny stones and then went back to sifting the sludge. Just then he came upon a big chunk of black rock and went to throw it out of his pan.

The old man said, "Hey, I like to collect those black rocks there. Mind if I have it?"

The young miner tossed the rock to the old miner with little regard. "Why do you collect these black stones, old-timer?"

"Oh, I just like 'em. Tell you what, if you find any more, toss 'em aside for me," the old man said.

The young miner laughed at the silly old man, "Sure, old man."

The old man went to town and sold the massive black diamonds for hundreds of thousands of dollars. Turns out, the young man didn't recognize the black diamonds. He threw away a fortune trying to find the white shiny ones.

Lots of people are like that young man. They don't know. They're judgmental, shortsighted, and inexperienced. They're confused and have no idea what's really important, valuable, and worth something. That's why you can't let your value be determined by

103

them. You've got to know you're a diamond whether others realize it or not.

I'm not saying to be arrogant. What I'm saying is what David Seamands says in his book, *Emotionally Damaged*. If you don't know who you are, and you're waiting around for someone to say you're worthy or valuable, you'll be miserable. You can get to the point where you don't even like being with yourself. If you don't like being with yourself, why would anyone else like being with you? You can become emotionally unavailable, distant, and angry, and you start giving off negative vibes. You have to arrest the attitude within yourself that looks outside for approval. You have to love yourself and get a sense of your own worth.

We all need to start seeing ourselves and others as being uniquely made by God, made to be who we individually are. Our world would be such a better place if we understood and accepted that fact. What we look like, what other people look like, what someone is gifted with, what someone else has, what we think someone else has—none of that matters.

You are a living, breathing, thinking, loving, gifted miracle made in the image of almighty God Himself. You're even more rare than a diamond. You are incredible!

If there's something in your mind telling you something else, throw it away. You are fearfully and wonderfully made, just as you are, and God loves you. You. Uniquely you. Why? Because God knows who and what you are. He crafted you to be precisely as you are. Ephesians 2:10 says you are an amazing workmanship of Christ Jesus. He knows you inside and out, and He loves you as you are. When you recognize this truth, you can stop worrying about what other people think about you.

Seeking the approval of others is a subtle temptation for all of us. As a pastor who preaches each Sunday, I find it tempting to come out and "wow" my congregation. I have to keep that attitude in check and make sure that what I'm doing is pleasing to God. My simple, silent prayer when I stand to preach is, "Only for Your pleasure, Father." My grandma used to say, "There's nothing worse than getting a whole lot of applause on earth and heaven ain't sayin' nothin' up there."

I could lose my mind trying to please people every week. Any given Sunday, I can look out over the church and see some people standing up praising God, full of the Spirit, and others looking at their watches, wanting me to shut up already so they can go watch the game. I can't worry about everybody; I've got to focus on pleasing God. That's all that matters.

The problematic pouch of people-pleasing can keep us from recognizing the powerful potential God has placed in each of us. People are fickle, but God is true and faithful. God made us the way we are to be uniquely who we are. If others don't understand that, then that's on them, not you. God wants you to live in power and confidence. He wants you to toss out the problematic pouch of people-pleasing today. Live for the applause of heaven, friend.

> GOD WANTS YOU TO LIVE IN POWER AND CONFIDENCE. HE WANTS YOU TO TOSS OUT THE PROBLEMATIC POUCH OF PEOPLE-PLEASING TODAY.

CHAPTER SIX
The Loathsome Luggage of Low Self-Esteem

"Do not think of yourself more highly than you ought, but rather think of yourself with sober judgment, in accordance with the faith God has distributed to each of you."
(Romans 12:3 NIV)

There is a feature of many old carnivals and amusement parks called the house of mirrors. If you've ever been in a house of mirrors, you know that along with the maze you must navigate there are also many concave and convex mirrors that distort your image in often grotesque, silly, or humorous ways. One mirror may make you appear taller than you are, or another may make you look short and round. If you're unfamiliar with the house of mirrors, perhaps you're more familiar with the Photobooth app on your iPhone or iPad where a tap of the screen or click of a mouse button twists your face into a swirl in the middle of your eye or gives you a forehead the size of your shoulders. The distorted images are, of course, all for fun and games, but what if we really saw ourselves that way?

Many of you reading this can imagine just that because you do this every time you look in the mirror. You view yourself in a distorted way. You think something is wrong with your hair, eyes, eyebrows, or ears. You think you're too big, too skinny, that your bones are too thin or too thick. You think you're ugly. You think no one likes you. The fact is, if we are not healed in our emotional life, we allow the devil to put us in a house of mirrors or to tap our screens and distort our image at will. This is particularly true with regards to how we view ourselves, our self-esteem.

ATTACKING ADS

Part of the problem with many of us in regards to our self-esteem is that we live in a world that attacks us. Day in and day out, images of what people "should" look like or what is considered attractive bombard us everywhere. We can't help but see these images of people—many of which look nothing like us. This is true mostly for minority ethnicities, but it seems especially true for African Americans. There are very few minority women with natural hair seen or celebrated on TV. On any given day, you are bombarded with thousands of images that look nothing like you and on a good day, if you're lucky, maybe a few that you can relate to. So much of our self-esteem is attacked as a matter of cultural bias and discrimination in the media. In our society, media and marketing has taken the initiative and defined what *they* perceive beauty to be.

> WE HAVEN'T LEARNED TO VALUE OURSELVES AND SEE OURSELVES THE WAY GOD SEES US. RATHER, WE TEND TO VIEW OURSELVES THE WAY MADISON AVENUE WANTS US TO SEE OURSELVES SO WE WILL BUY THEIR PRODUCTS.

Many of us internalize these differences and attack ourselves emotionally and mentally when we look in the mirror because we haven't learned to value ourselves and see ourselves the way God sees us. Rather, we tend to view ourselves the way Madison Avenue wants us to see ourselves so we will buy their products.

That's what TV is all about—selling products. The shows are only there to sell you stuff. That's where the term *soap opera* came from. They were stories sponsored and sometimes even created by soap companies for housewives so that those housewives would buy their cleaning products. The concept was so successful that it expanded into what we have today. Sports shows are created to sell razor blades and pick-up trucks to men. Cooking and home shows are created to sell furniture, appliances, food, and housewares. Cartoons and kid shows sell Disney vacations, video games, and other toys; and dramas sell hair products, new cars, jewelry, clothes, and services.

Even if you buy all these things and do everything they tell you to do, companies have figured out how to use perceived and planned obsolescence to make sure you replace your stuff as soon as possible. Ever notice how shoe heels and men's ties and lapels go from skinny to wide and then wide to skinny every few years? How styles go from tight to loose? It's gradual, but it's all calculated to keep you buying things and always feeling like you don't have the latest and greatest or you're not good enough.

Many of us have these distorted images of ourselves because we fail to see ourselves as God sees us: as beloved of God and joint-heirs with Christ. As a result, we go through life with low self-esteem. This comes not only from advertising but also from the adversary, the devil's tricks and the mental and emotional games people play when they put us down. When our self-esteem is attacked, we have a discounted view of our personal worth, and how we see ourselves dictates how we allow others to treat us.

In this chapter, I want to take a look at the loathsome luggage of low self-esteem and how it impacts us and weighs us down on our journey. We have enough to deal with in life without having to carry this weight around. I want to explore not only where we picked up this bag, but also how to get rid of it once and for all.

SHAMEFUL SELF-ESTEEM

If you want to know how the loathsome luggage of low self-esteem impacts us, think about why some people allow others to mistreat them. It is usually because that person has low self-esteem. If we see a person who carries himself or herself in a way that is shameful, it is likely because he or she has self-esteem issues. If you see a person who abuses himself or herself, it is often due to low self-esteem. If a person does not take care of himself or herself physically—exercise and eat right—it is occasionally the result of not feeling worthy of being protected and cared for.

If people attribute anything they do well to luck rather than their own actions, low self-esteem is often at the root. If a person is unable to look others in the eye, it is usually because of low self-esteem. If a person walks around with her head hanging low or shoulders slumped over, you can reasonably expect that low self-esteem plagues her.

In fact, therapist Mark Tyrrell offers this list of characteristics that people who suffer from low self-esteem generally display:

- Social withdrawal
- Anxiety and emotional turmoil
- Lack of social skills and self-confidence
- Depression and/or bouts of sadness
- Less social conformity
- Eating disorders
- Inability to accept compliments
- An inability to be fair to yourself
- Accentuating the negative
- Exaggerated concern over what you imagine other people think
- Self-neglect
- Treating yourself badly but not other people
- Worrying whether you have treated others badly
- Reluctance to take on challenges
- Reluctance to put yourself first or anywhere
- Reluctance to trust your own opinion
- Expecting little out of life for yourself[7]

Does any of that sound familiar? If so, you may be carrying around the loathsome luggage of low self-esteem. Later on, we'll take a look at some biblical characters and how their low self-esteem issues impacted their lives and their relationships with God, but let's first deal with ourselves.

My goal in this chapter is to help us develop a healthy self-esteem, as Christ would have us possess. Together, we'll take a look at the problems of low self-esteem, the producers of low self-esteem, and the prescription for true self-esteem.

Before we begin, however, let me clarify something. There are two different types of self-esteem: negative and positive. The negative type is what most people would know as human pride. Human pride is a self-centered, personal appraisal based on our effort apart from God's evaluation. This type of esteem says, "I am what I do." If we land the right job, we feel more valuable because our self-image is based on what we do. If we can dunk a basketball, we feel good about ourselves. If we get into our first choice of school, we have strong self-esteem. This type of self-esteem also says, "I am what I have," which implies our possessions define who we are. We feel valuable because we own things; our value is based on superficial symbols of success. People who believe this go into great debt to have things they often cannot afford. This mindset will have you buying what you want and begging for what you need.

This type of self-esteem may also say, "I am what others think about me." As we discussed in our last chapter, people who base their self-esteem on others' opinions fall victim to people-pleasing. Finally, this type of self-esteem may also say, "I am how I look." Although there's nothing wrong with wanting to look presentable, when our whole lives are consumed with our outward appearances, we are defining ourselves via human pride. This negative form of self-esteem is narcissistic in nature in that it's an excessive or erotic interest in one's status or appearance.

This human pride is not the type of self-esteem God wants us to have. In fact, the Bible warns us against being too invested in human pride, as it can take our eyes off God and lead to ones fall (Proverbs16:18). If you only have strong self-esteem because you can dunk a basketball, what happens if you damage your knee and can't do that anymore? If you're great because you live in a big, fancy house or drive a luxury car, what happens if you lose those things or go bankrupt?

If you base your self-esteem on worldly praise, what happens when worldly praise goes away? The ESPN film *Broke* chronicles the lives of numerous NFL players who declared bankruptcy after once having been multimillionaires. They heard the roar of the crowds, achieved fame, and commanded the highest of salaries; but now they have nothing but a life of memories and regrets. If your self-esteem depends on what you have, I can assure you it is resting on shaky ground.

The type of self-esteem God wants us to have is based on God's evaluation of our lives. As believers, we should base our self-esteem on what God says about us, not on worldly possessions or opinions. Romans 12:3 says, "Do not think of yourself more highly than you ought, but rather think of yourself with sober judgment, in accordance with the faith God has distributed to each of you" (NIV). This verse emphasizes that we ought not to think too highly of ourselves nor too lowly. *Sober judgment* means "accurately" or "with balance." Therefore, our views of ourselves should be balanced with accuracy.

So many times when we try to build our self-esteem, we find ourselves swinging like a pendulum. Many people over the years have misunderstood how self-esteem works. They once believed that if a child was being a bully, it was because that child had low self-esteem. Today, they realize the opposite is usually true. Often the bully has too much esteem and entitlement and is bullying people because he thinks of himself as better than his victims. Likewise, some people believe if you merely give others compliments, it will improve their self-esteem. In fact, it might only reinforce negative feelings, especially if they see you saying nice things to everyone all the time.

Strong, positive self-esteem can be built only through the application of truth and honesty. Jesus isn't interested in filling you up with platitudes to make you feel good; He is interested in helping you understand the truth of how He created you with unique and powerful design and purpose.

CRIPPLING POTENTIAL

Many biblical characters carried the loathsome luggage of low self-esteem. In Numbers 13:33, we read the account of the twelve leaders Moses sent out as spies into Canaan. It's important to note these men were leaders of the twelve tribes of Israel. They were men who held positions of authority in the new nation. People looked to them for guidance and advice and placed their faith in them. After spying out the land, Joshua and Caleb said, "We can take them." Yet the other ten came back and reported, "We saw the Nephilim [the descendants of Anak come from the Nephilim]. We seemed like grasshoppers in our own eyes, and we looked the same to them" (NIV).

Can you imagine how intimidated these men were? Look at their description of the inhabitants of Canaan. They said they felt like grasshoppers next to them! Certainly not all the people of Canaan were giants or Joshua and Caleb wouldn't have reported as they did. The Israelite leaders had a distorted image of themselves and their people, which they embraced and believed over the promise Moses told them God made: to give them victory over the land. This verse shows how low self-esteem cripples our potential.

The Israelite leaders not only believed they were grasshoppers compared to the men of Canaan, but they also falsely believed that the men of Canaan thought the Israelites were as little as grasshoppers as well. Joshua 2:8-11 shows how the Canaanites really felt: "Before the spies went to sleep that night, Rahab went up on the roof to talk with them. 'I know the LORD has given you this land,' she told them. 'We are all afraid of you. Everyone in the land is living in terror. For we have heard how the LORD made a dry path for you through the Red Sea when you left Egypt. And we know what you did to Sihon and Og, the two Amorite kings east of the Jordan River, whose people you completely destroyed. No wonder our hearts have melted in fear! No one has the courage to fight after hearing such things. For the LORD your God is the supreme God of the heavens above and the earth below' " (NLT).

The spies had a wrong assessment of themselves. The Canaanites were so frightened of the Israelites that they were afraid to fight them. The Israelites could have walked into the land and taken it without a battle if they believed what Moses told them. If they viewed themselves as God saw them, they could have spared themselves the forty years of wandering in the desert, which happened between the time the first set of twelve spies went in the Book of Numbers and the different set of two spies went in the Book of Joshua. God had to let that entire disbelieving generation die out before He could get them to have the confidence to finally move into the Promised Land.

This is how it is when you have low self-esteem. It will always cripple your potential. With low self-esteem, you will never maximize your impact or live up to the level God wants for you. Low self-esteem lowers the ceiling on your life. If the ceiling is low, how high can you climb? As long as you go through life with a perspective of your life that is less than God's perspective, you always will have a low ceiling. With that low ceiling, it doesn't matter how much effort you put into something; you are limited. Even when you think you're achieving, you can only ascend as high as that ceiling.

There are many people who will read this who are living below where God wants them to live. You may not have what you want in your life because you do not see yourself as God sees you; you do not believe God can do for you what He promises. You see yourself as a grasshopper, as insignificant. You see yourself as someone who cannot achieve. God sees you as triumphant, as the apple of His eye, but you have such low self-esteem that you have to walk with your head down to keep from hitting it on your low ceiling.

God has given you gifts and abilities to live your life to its full potential, but you have to have the confidence to use those gifts. You have to have the confidence to march into the land. If you don't, like the Israelites, you risk running around the desert for forty years as well.

IMPACTING RELATIONSHIPS

In addition to crippling potential, carrying the luggage of low self-esteem can also impact our relationships. First, it impacts our relationship with the Omnipotent. If we do not believe God can love us because we are so unlovable, we then try to figure out how we can make ourselves more worthy of His love; but this goes against God's grace. There is nothing we can do to impress God. As a matter of fact, there is nothing we can do to make God love us any more and conversely, there is nothing we can do to make Him love us any less. Our value is not based on what we do; our value is based on what God did for us.

Your value to God is not based on how many people you win to Jesus or how many times a week you go to church. It's not based on anything except His blood and your relationship to Him through His Son's death, burial, and resurrection. When you start to think there is something you can do to make God love you more than He already demonstrated by giving His Son for you, you negate the true meaning of God's amazing grace. "For it is by grace you have been saved, through faith—and this is not from yourselves, it is the gift of God—not by works, so that no one can boast" (Ephesians 2:8-9, NIV).

Second, low self-esteem impacts our relationships with others. Low self-esteem can cause us to withdraw into isolation. We pull ourselves away from relationships, from friendships, and from being involved with others because we don't see ourselves as we should and think others don't like us or don't want to be around us. Do you know anyone like that? People who won't go out or who always have some excuse why they can't do something? The real reason is they don't believe other people want to be around them. And guess what? That may be true.

No one wants to be around toxic people because their conversations take on their negativity. If you ever listen to people with low self-esteem, it oozes into their conversations—how something can't happen or won't happen for them, how everybody is against them, how no one likes them, how no one wants to be around them. Eventually, you will hear some type of defeatist dialogue, and before long you'll start wanting to move away from them, too. Their negativity becomes self-fulfilling prophecy.

Third, low self-esteem can sabotage our ministries. When you have low self-esteem and you're trying to please God through your works, it becomes a chore done out of duty and obligation rather than out of gratitude for the gift of grace and salvation that God has given you.

This is a potential risk for those who serve in full-time vocational ministry. When we're engaged in serving the Lord but there is no joy or excitement in the work, we need to take a moment to refocus and get right our hearts and minds. When you're trying to prove to God you're good enough, you work hard and don't care how long it takes because you've got something to prove.

CAUSES OF LOW SELF-ESTEEM

Our sense of self-esteem is the result of personal experiences. We are each born with a variety of physical, mental, emotional, and spiritual attributes. These not only include our capacity to learn and respond, but they also include our handicaps, deformities, limitations, and so forth. These are the results of being born into a broken world. Some of us are fortunate to be born to loving, wise parents, and some of us weren't so fortunate. Some of us were born into stable homes, and some not so. Some of us were born into strong, healthy families, and some into dysfunctional ones.

The things we've done or gone through impact our lives in ways that influence our self-esteem. Hardships, injuries, and difficulties hit us throughout our lives. If we're not guided through these things by someone who loves us, we can find ourselves at forty, fifty, and sixty years old still dealing with stuff that happened to us when we were children. Often, because we haven't addressed and dealt with our stuff, these experiences can continue to have a negative impact on our self-esteem.

Everyone experiences adversities in their lives. Sometimes, when I tell people this, they initially think I'm being cold. I'm not; it's reality. You have to understand that everyone has had something happen in their lives that they have to deal with—something hurtful, evil, wrong, or painful. The thing that happened to me is different than what happened to you. The fact that something happened to you doesn't make you unique. It certainly doesn't mean anyone is going to treat you special because of it. In fact, there's always someone who had it much worse than you.

We've all endured negative things. In most cases, there's nothing you can do about it. It's a bit like a birthmark; no matter how much you scrub, it's not going anywhere. At some point, you have to come to terms with it. You may have come into the world with it, but it does not determine your value.

We have to make up our minds that we are not going to allow these things to continue to impact our lives. We have to get beyond the superficial stuff of life. If you have a big nose, that's your nose. If you have a pointy chin, that's your chin. If you're short, tall, slim, or not so much, that's you. You can work to change it or accept it, but don't change to please other people.

A second cause of low self-esteem is our social experience. The totality of our experiences and the influences in our lives and relationships to this point in time has an impact on our self-esteem. The major influencers in our formative years are our parents, then later it becomes our significant others—for better or worse. That's why, as parents and adults, one of the worse things we can do to a child is say negative, mean, cruel words. Even when said jokingly, our words can have a devastating impact on young minds. You may be choking seeds that were planted in them, giving rise to low self-esteem in their minds. Someone calls a child dumb or stupid or fat or ugly, and that child may believe it because the person who said it is supposed to be a loved one or a trusted family member. That thought goes inside them and waits for others to come along later and feed it, and before long they are hauling around the loathsome luggage of low self-esteem tossed on them by others.

Another cause of low self-esteem is the words we say to ourselves when we're struggling with the grievous grip of guilt I wrote about in Chapter Four. Sometimes we do things we feel bad about and beat ourselves up because we don't know how to deal with the guilt. Sometimes the damage we leave in our own minds is not unlike the damage that comes when other people beat us up with words. None of us are perfect. If we feel we have to be perfect in order to have healthy self-esteem, then we're liable to be stuck in low self-esteem for as long as we feel that way.

Finally, in that we are constantly in spiritual warfare, our enemy Satan goes to no limits in seeking to damage our sense of self-esteem. Satan wants to exploit every emotional infirmity you have. He wants to reinforce every feeling of inferiority, worthlessness, or inadequacy you feel.

Satan belittles all people with lies, accusations, and soul-destroying distortions of the truth because his goal is to keep you from living a victorious life in Christ. He doesn't want you victorious because he doesn't want you embracing your true identity in Christ or drawing others to God. He wants to make those who love God look bad to the world. He wants to make the Christian life look unappealing, unpleasant, boring, and burdensome. He wants to make serving him look cool, powerful, and preferred. He doesn't want you happy; he wants you miserable, if for no other reason than to make God look bad.

All of these areas are where we pick up the loathsome luggage of low self-esteem, but the good news is that God has the prescription for true self-esteem.

THE PRESCRIPTION FOR TRUE SELF-ESTEEM

So what does God say we need to do to have proper, strong self-esteem? How do you begin this journey, this healing process toward developing a healthy, positive self-esteem? What is the path toward deliverance?

It begins with what we say to ourselves.

First, we have to understand that self-denigration and self-hate do not equal humility. Many of us tend to say things about ourselves that, in reality, belittle us. We believe we are being humble, but it's not humility to put ourselves down. There's nothing honorable about hurting yourself any more than it is honorable to hurt someone else. In fact, many of us say things to ourselves we would never say to another person. We call ourselves stupid for common mistakes like forgetting our car keys or missing an appointment or getting an answer wrong on a test, but we would never call a friend stupid who did the same thing. We can be so cruel to ourselves.

If you're going to heal your self-esteem, it starts with changing what you say to yourself because how you think dictates your whole life. Proverbs 23:7 says, "For as he thinketh in his heart, so is he." That means you have to learn to think right about yourself to be right in your self-esteem. Do you get it? The word *esteem* means "to honor, to respect, to like, to regard highly." If you want to be good, honorable, respected, and regarded highly, you have to think that way about yourself. As you think, so are you. In other words, you will never live any higher than your thoughts of yourself.

Jesus also says something interesting. In response to the question, "What is the greatest commandment?" Jesus answered, "Love the Lord your God with all your heart and with all your soul and with all your mind. This is the first and greatest commandment. And the second is like it: Love your neighbor as yourself. All the Law and the Prophets hang on these two commandments" (Matthew 22:37-40, NIV).

All the books of the Law and the Prophets—in other words, the whole Old Testament—hang on these two commands. Sounds pretty important, right? We might want to make sure we get this one right. How can you honor God's Word and obey what He says if you don't love yourself? How do you love your neighbor if you don't love yourself?

No, this is not a loophole to get out of loving your neighbor. You can't say, "Oh, I love my neighbor as I love myself; I just don't love myself much." A lot of people may actually think like that, but they're missing what God is saying. God wants you to have a healthy self-respect, self-love, self-honor, and self-regard. Then He wants you to have a similar honor, love, regard, and respect for others. The fact is we cannot love others freely, with any hidden agendas, until we love ourselves, accept ourselves, and are at peace with ourselves; but we can do this because God loves and accepts us.

118

Our value is not in what we do, where we work, how much we have, the level of our education, our appearance, or our abilities. The basis of our self-esteem is who God says we are. You have to know this, believe this, live this. If you want to change what you become, you have to change what you believe about yourself.

EIGHT AFFIRMATIONS

There are eight affirmations that will enthrone this truth in your life and help you change the way you think about yourself. An affirmation is a statement of truth. As such, speak these affirmations out loud to yourself in order to affirm a truth God has said about you in His Word.

The first of these eight affirmations is, "God loves me so deeply." Say that to yourself right now. Say it like you mean it and believe it because it is true. God indeed loves you so deeply. No matter what someone else may do or say, God loves you more than you realize. Someone may hurt you, make you cry, or make you feel bad, but you're going to bounce back because God loves you deeply, intimately, and unconditionally. There's no need to sit around feeling sorry for yourself anymore, to be depressed, or to have negative thoughts because God loves you so deeply. Yes, He does!

The proof of this is found in 1 John 4: "This is how God showed his love among us: He sent his one and only Son into the world that we might live through him. . . . And so we know and rely on the love God has for us" (verses 9, 16, NIV).

The second affirmation that can heal your self-esteem is, "God honors me so highly." Say that out loud now. Say it until you feel the truth of it break through to your soul. It's based on 1 John 3:2: "Dear friends, now we are children of God, and what we will be has not yet been made known. But we know that when Christ appears, we shall be like him, for we shall see him as he is" (NIV). Do you see the way God honors you in this verse? You are His child. That makes you an heir of God and a joint-heir with Christ. What an amazing honor! You not only are a child and heir of God, but you shall be like Him when Christ returns.

The third affirmation to say aloud is, "God values me so completely." This affirmation is based on the truth found in Romans 5:6-8: "You see, at just the right time, when we were still powerless, Christ died for the ungodly. Very rarely will anyone die for a righteous person, though for a good person someone might possibly dare to die. But God demonstrates his own love for us in this: While we were still sinners, Christ died for us" (NIV). Your value is not based on symbols of success, on the designer clothes you may wear, on some achievement or accomplishment. Your value is based on the fact that God honors you and gave His only Son to die for you.

The fourth affirmation to say aloud to yourself is, "God provides for me so fully," based on Romans 8:31-34: "What, then, shall we say in response to these things? If God is for us, who can be against us? He who did not spare his own Son, but gave him up for us all—how will he not also, along with him, graciously give us all things? Who will bring any charge against those whom God has chosen? It is God who justifies. Who then is the one who condemns? No one. Christ Jesus who died—more than that, who was raised to life—is at the right hand of God and is also interceding for us" (NIV).

Do you see that truth in those verses? God will give you all things. Jesus Christ is at the right hand of the Father interceding on your behalf. He is your advocate and chief intercessor. When Satan brings charges against you, God has you covered. He's been praying you through. That's the reason why you've come through what you went through and you're still here: He's providing for you.

Psalms 139 gives us a fifth affirmation to say aloud, "God knows me completely and thoroughly. God plans for me so carefully." Say that out loud to yourself, then read verses 1-6, which prove it's true: "You have searched me, LORD, and you know me. You know when I sit and when I rise; you perceive my thoughts from afar. You discern my going out and my lying down; you are familiar with all my ways. Before a word is on my tongue you, LORD, know it completely. You hem me in behind and before, and you lay your hand upon me. Such knowledge is too wonderful for me, too lofty for me to attain" (NIV).

God has searched you, and He sees you. He knows all of what you're about and accepts you. He sees what you're thinking before you even think it. He knows what you're going to say before you say it. He's already planned for you. He's already figured it out. When you think about it, that kind of care is overwhelmingly wonderful; and get this—He places His hand on you. His hand of blessing covers your life, and no one can remove it. No weapon the devil forms shall prosper against you. No plans of any enemies shall come to fruition against you. Why? Because God has already planned for your victory.

The sixth affirmation you should say out loud is, "God delights in me so abundantly." The proof of this affirmation is found in Zephaniah 3:17: "The LORD your God is with you, the Mighty Warrior who saves. He will take great delight in you; in his love he will no longer rebuke you, but will rejoice over you with singing" (NIV).

Do you see why your self-esteem should be strong? It says God takes great delight over you. You know what that means? It means He likes you. *He likes you!* You know you may only love some people because you're supposed to love them; but when you say you love someone *and* you like them, that's something else. What about those people you love and delight in having around? That's how God feels about you. You delight God. How can you not like yourself when God delights in you? It's wonderful to be loved, but being loved *and* liked is incomparable. Say that affirmation aloud again: "God delights in me so abundantly."

A seventh affirmation to help heal our self-esteem and enthrone the values that God wants us to have in our lives is, "God accepts me completely." This is found in Ephesians 1:6: "To the praise of the glory of his grace, wherein he hath made us accepted in the beloved." There's nothing you can do to get God to love you, approve of you, or accept you. Jesus already did it all on the cross. You are accepted in Christ. You're approved. We like to hear that, don't we? When we apply for a mortgage or a car loan, we like to hear the loan officer say we're approved. We've qualified. Jesus made you qualified, approved, and accepted. You've been admitted to God's family. Welcome!

The eighth and final affirmation is, "God completes me thoroughly." A lot of us need to say this one *very* loud. So many of us are looking for someone else to come and complete us, but we need to know that only God completes us. Colossians 2:10 says, "Ye are complete in him." I didn't get completed when I married my wife, Cleo. We have a wonderful marriage, but she didn't get completed when she married me, either. We were both already complete in Christ. When two complete people come together in marriage, that's a good thing.

When two incomplete people come together, that can be a real problem. Two incomplete people will always find frustration because they each are looking for the other person to provide what he or she is incapable of providing.

The only completeness comes from our relationship with God through Christ Jesus. You could win the lottery tonight and, without God, you still wouldn't be complete and would continue to have self-image issues because money doesn't solve any problems or complete you. Money, cars, houses, fame—none of it completes a person. God has placed a hole in every person that can only be filled by Him. Saint Augustine of Hippo spoke on the restlessness and incompleteness that frustrates humanity when they try to live separate and apart from God: "Thou has made us for Thyself, O Lord, and our heart is restless until it finds rest in Thee."[8]

So you are confronted with choices. Will you continue to listen and believe the distorted messages from childhood? Will you continue to look at yourself through the mirror of other people's opinions? Will you continue to allow Satan's lies and accusations to determine how you feel about yourself? Or will you begin to listen to, believe in, and act upon what God says about your worth and value?

Santa Claus, the Tooth Fairy, and the Easter Bunny aren't the only lies our child-like minds accept. When we are children, our minds accept all types of things we hear. All we, as children, have to do is hear something one time, and we can believe it forever without even questioning it; but as we get older, we have to tell ourselves the truth over and over again to get our minds to adjust to it. The little child in you can be fooled. If you're walking around feeling bad about yourself, full of self-esteem issues, not liking or loving yourself, it's often because as a child you heard some lies and believed them.

You've got to recognize that the child in you wasn't all-knowing, didn't understand everything correctly, and was lied to. You need to tell that child you've got it now and you're not going to let him or her control your emotions anymore. You have to correct the misinformation in your head if you want to be free from the loathsome luggage of low self-esteem. Besides, living your life through other people's eyes is exhausting. It's also completely unnecessary. Living your life based on Satan's input is setting yourself up for true disaster.

The key to making the right choice is the practice of renewing your mind. That's what these affirmations are about. You must retrain your thinking to get away from the old ruts that form in your thoughts.

Psychologists tell us that old thoughts are like water hitting a rock over time and wearing a groove into it. In time, any water that hits that rock will run to that groove. Likewise, any thoughts we have, if we have developed negative patterns of thinking, will run into those negative grooves. The only way to stop it is to interrupt the flow, to literally force a new groove into the rock. The Bible shows us how to renew our minds in Romans 12:2: "Don't copy the behavior and customs of this world, but let God transform you into a new person by changing the way you think. Then you will learn to know God's will for you, which is good and pleasing and perfect" (NLT).

We change the way we think—the groove that old thinking has worn into our minds—by changing our customs and behavior.

When we recite the affirmations we learned in this chapter, we force our minds to view the world through a different set of values. We change the programming coming at us all day long through TV, music, and movies.

When we apply God's Word to our lives, we find new power, new wisdom, new ways of viewing the world, and we come to see ourselves as God sees us. When we do, we no longer struggle with self-esteem issues because we know who we are and that we're loved, approved, complete, accepted, valued, delighted in, provided for, planned for, and honored. When we know this, we can toss that loathsome luggage of low self-esteem overboard and keep it out of our lives for good.

TIED TO STAKES

Do you know what they do to keep a circus elephant from running away? They tie a metal chain to a collar around the mighty elephant's leg and tie it to a small wooden peg that's hammered into the ground. The ten-foot-tall, ten-thousand-pound hulk could easily snap the chain, uproot the wooden peg, and escape to freedom; but it does not do that. In fact, it does not even try.

It's because when the elephant was a baby, its trainers used exactly the same methods. A chain was tied around its leg, and the other end of the chain was tied to a metal stake in the ground. The chain and peg were strong enough for the baby elephant. When it tried to break away, the metal chain would pull it back; but the chain would cut into the skin on the elephant's leg, making it bleed and creating a wound that would hurt the baby elephant even more. Soon, the baby elephant realized it was futile and too painful to try and escape. It stopped trying!

Now the big circus elephant with a chain tied around its leg remembers the pain it felt as a baby, and it does not try to break away. It does not matter that a wooden peg has replaced the metal stake. It does not matter that the two-hundred-pound baby is now a ten-thousand-pound powerhouse. However, the elephant's belief prevails, and his spirit and sense of self-esteem is broken.

We are like the elephant in many ways. We are tied to stakes that keep us from moving forward with a healthy and victorious life. Often our stakes are fears that we learned when we were young. Many of us grew up on an unhealthy diet of negativities: "Don't do that!" or "You can't do that!" or "You are no good!" so we stop ourselves from aiming high. We say, "I can't do it because . . ." and fill in our favorite default excuse.

These self-limiting beliefs are rooted in the sphere of our self-image and become chains that stop us from trying. Circumstances change, and wooden pegs replace metal poles. We don't realize that when we stop trying we are giving up.

As adults, we often play the role of elephant trainer—as parents, teachers, colleagues, or friends. When that happens, remember to handle your baby elephants with care! Don't be critical. Don't be negative. Don't belittle them. Don't chain them to a peg. All of these things can ruin one's self-esteem and productivity. Remember, we all have the strength of an elephant. Don't let a mere chain or wooden peg hold you back from a victorious life. It's a good idea to recognize what or who is holding you back. Break the shackles of your self-limiting beliefs, and recognize the strengths that lie within you. Let Christ set you free—today!

BREAK THE SHACKLES OF YOUR SELF-LIMITING BELIEFS, AND RECOGNIZE THE STRENGTHS THAT LIE WITHIN YOU. LET CHRIST SET YOU FREE—TODAY!

CHAPTER 7
The Frightening Flip Bag of Fear

"Fear not . . . for thou hast found favour with God."
(Luke 1:30)

A man tells the story of vacationing with his family at his father-in-law's house in Fort Lauderdale, Florida. Earlier in the year, there had been a report of a shark attack in Florida, so he asked his father-in-law if the waters were safe.

"Oh yeah," his father-in-law said. "That was further up north. Everything is fine down here."

So the next day the man planned a day at the beach with his wife and nine-year-old daughter; but when they got to the beach, it started raining. They decided to go look at some open houses instead.

On their way back the rain stopped, so they headed to the nearest beach, Del Ray Beach. The family thought they were lucky to find parking and be the first ones there. They put out their beach towels, and the man and his daughter jumped in the warm ocean to swim.

Soon after, a lone stranger approached the wife on the shore and told her, "Someone reported sharks twenty minutes away." The wife began shouting for her family to get out of the water. The husband came out to see what was wrong.

"Sharks, twenty minutes away! Get out of the water!" his wife yelled frantically to their daughter.

"Twenty minutes away? Twenty minutes by what? Car? plane? shark swim?" The comment seemed absurd to him. "Well," he joked, "since we've got at least twenty minutes, let her swim for nineteen. The water is crystal clear, I can see to the bottom. There's nothing out there."

"Just get out the water, please," she insisted. "GET OUT OF THE WATER!" she yelled to her daughter, irritating her husband.

The girl got upset because it was the first time at the beach since they arrived, and it was very hot. "It's okay," the man told the girl. "You can swim."

"If it's okay, why is no one on the beach?" his wife reasoned.

"Because it just stopped raining. We're the first ones here. Relax."

Then they noticed a man struggling with a large fishing pole about one hundred yards down the beach. "See," his wife said, "I bet he caught a shark. Get out of the water, baby!" she ordered her daughter again.

The man laughed. "He's snagged on something. Look at his pole. It's bent in half."

But moments later, they noticed a giant fish on the shore. Even one hundred yards away, the man could see it was a shark. He quickly pulled his daughter from the water, and they all ran down the shore. Sure enough, the fisherman had caught a six-foot bull shark.

The most frightening part was that when the fisherman released the shark, it vanished in only two feet of water. Even though the water was perfectly clear, he couldn't see the shark. He and his daughter had been swimming in water at least twice that depth.

When the family returned to their father-in-law's home, they saw a news report that showed the man and his daughter had been surrounded by hundreds of lethal sharks. It turned out that when they went looking at houses, they had unknowingly driven north to the area his father-in-law warned them about.

Although they used to swim in the Atlantic Ocean regularly, it's been more than ten years since the family has gone swimming there. Even though nothing happened that day, fear still controls them to this day.

IN THE BLINK OF AN EYE

If you've never heard of a flip bag, it might be because it is relatively new. It is a strong, nylon satchel, about the size of a large shopping bag, that can ball up and fit into a little bag so you can carry it on you at all times without having to carry a heavy bag. The idea of the flip bag is similar to the idea of packable coats, which fold up into little bags you can throw in a backpack in case the weather suddenly changes and it starts to rain or gets chilly. The idea behind the flip bag is its ability to take on a new shape and size quickly and easily. One minute you may forget you have it, and the next minute it's holding all your stuff.

> IN THE BLINK OF AN EYE, YOUR WORLD CAN CHANGE OR BE THREATENED. FEAR HAS A WAY OF GRIPPING YOU BY THE THROAT AND MAKING YOU GASP FOR AIR.

Fear can be that way. One minute you're doing fine, all is right with the world. The next minute, you're consumed by a fear you didn't realize you had or didn't realize was creeping up on you. The experience can be devastating. In the blink of an eye, your world can change or be threatened. Fear has a way of gripping you by the throat and making you gasp for air.

Ever have the phone ring in the middle of the night? You don't usually get calls that late. You check the caller ID, and it's the relative who takes care of your elderly mom. The veins in your neck constrict as you dread answering, trying not to imagine what terrible news it could be.

Have you ever been on your way to a get-together and gotten lost (especially before the days of GPS or when you have your device but don't have a signal)? You find yourself in a strange part of town and don't recognize your surroundings. Maybe you got off at the wrong stop on the bus or the train. Maybe you got off on the wrong exit on the highway because you were running out of gas. But you can't find a gas station; you can't find anything, not even how to get back on the freeway.

Have you ever entered your home and thought you were alone,

only to hear a strange noise? The threat arrests your mind and heart, your pulse quickens, and you enter what psychologists call "fight or flight."

What do you fear the most in life? Most people fear something—the loss of life, the loss of health, the loss of family members. This chapter is about dealing with that frightening flip bag of fear. It's about dealing with the sudden awareness of danger and threat that pops out of nowhere and consumes you. It's about how to handle fear that interrupts your day, your thoughts, your plans, and your schedule.

FEAR NOT

The person we will study is Mary, the mother of Jesus. According to biblical scholars, Mary was likely between fourteen and sixteen years old when she was visited by the angel Gabriel and given shocking news that would forever change her life. The news Gabriel delivered was scandalous. The news was not only shameful for Mary and her family, but it could have been life threatening. Mary's life was going to change in ways she never imagined, and there was a lot for her to fear; but we can learn a few lessons from her story to help us cope with the fear we encounter before it takes over our lives.

Mary's story is in the Book of Luke. One of the things we learn is that Mary wasn't the only scared person at that time; quite a few people were also frightened. It's interesting to note what the angel told each one of them when they were faced with their fears with a simple two-word command: "Fear not." The words are spoken first to the priest Zacharias in the Temple when Gabriel appeared to him to announce that his barren wife would conceive a child in Luke 1:13, "Fear not, Zacharias." Next, they are spoken to Mary. When Gabriel appeared to her in Luke 1:30, he said, "Fear not, Mary."

The apostle Matthew tells us that when Joseph, Mary's fiancé, realized she was pregnant and it wasn't his child she was carrying, he planned to break off their engagement privately to avoid embarrassing her, but the angel of the Lord came to him and said, "Joseph, thou son of David, *fear not* to take unto thee Mary thy wife: for that which is conceived in her is of the Holy Ghost" (Matthew 1:20, italics added). Beyond that, on the night of Jesus's birth, the angel of the Lord came to the shepherds in the field and told them, "Fear not, for behold I bring you good tidings of great joy, which shall be to all people" (Luke 2:10).

If we look at the message Mary was given, we can get a sense of the types of fear she faced. The angel Gabriel gave her a threefold message: You're going to be pregnant even though you are a virgin; Joseph, your fiancé, will not be the father; and your child will be none other than the Son of God. Remember, Mary is only a teenager when all this happens to her. Imagine the fears she surely experienced:

- Fear of the unknown: "What is going to happen to me?"
- Fear of inadequacy: "How am I going to be able to do this?"
- Fear of change: "Will my life ever be the same?"
- Fear of people: "Will people believe me or will they criticize me or reject me?"

That's a lot for anyone to handle, let alone a young girl. After all, this news wasn't only going to affect her, it was going to affect her family, her friends, her fiancé, and her future. Whatever plans she had for herself and her soon-to-be husband were going to be shelved because God had other plans.

If you examine Gabriel's words closely, he uttered a terribly scary pronouncement, even though he started with, "Hail, thou that art highly favored, the Lord is with thee" (Luke 1:28). Mary was trying to figure out what kind of greeting this was. She wasn't from the high society of Israel. Her family was part of the average working class. You can tell she was perplexed by her response to Gabriel: "She was troubled at his saying, and cast in her mind what manner of salutation this should be" (verse 29). Mary was trying to figure out who this person was. Where'd he come from? How did he know her? Why did he talk to her like that, calling her "highly favored"?

Then Gabriel began telling her how God had chosen her to carry His Son and she was to call Him Jesus. Mary asked the one direct question on her mind: *How can I be pregnant when I haven't had any involvement with any man, let alone Joseph?* Imagine being Mary, a teenager who is told by a stranger that she was pregnant while still being a virgin and would give birth to a son—but not just any son. Oh no! She would birth the Son of God. Imagine Mary trying to understand Gabriel's explanation of the situation: "The Holy Ghost shall come upon thee, and the power of the Highest shall overshadow thee: therefore also that holy thing which shall be born of thee shall be called the Son of God" (verse 35).

That's pretty scary stuff!

We've probably heard the story so many times that we don't really think about the words, but the words are significant. The power of the Highest will "overshadow" you. You will bear a "Holy thing." Then Gabriel added that Mary's cousin Elizabeth, who was an old lady well past the age of being able to conceive, was also pregnant and would serve as proof that what he was telling her would come to pass.

If we look closely at how Mary handled this situation, we will gain some insight into how we can handle our own frightening situations. Mary's answer to Gabriel after hearing this pronouncement was simply, "Behold the handmaiden of the Lord. Be it unto me according to thy word" (verse 38). You know what that was like? Mary, in typical teenager fashion, said, "Okay, if you say so."

And that was it—for a minute.

It feels as if no time had passed when we jump to the next verse, but you have to learn to read a bit between the lines to understand what really happened. Verse 39 says, "And Mary arose *in those days*, and went . . . with haste, into a city of Juda" (italics added). In other words, Mary didn't do it right away. It took her some time, some days in fact, to digest this information before she decided to check on her cousin to confirm Gabriel's story. During that time, she likely thought over what Gabriel said and began to develop the faith necessary to move past her fears.

SNAP SHUT YOUR FEARS

The flip bag I refer to in this chapter usually comes with a little snap on it. To keep the flip bag of fear from taking up too much space in our lives and overwhelming us, we have to fold the bag up tight, stick it in its pouch, and snap it shut.

We can learn to snap shut that flip bag of fear by focusing on several key elements of Mary's interaction with Gabriel.

First, Luke 1:26-28 teaches us to fasten our faith to the assurance of God's presence. This is found in the first thing Gabriel said. Mary had to think about it over and over again to get her mind to accept it, but it's true: "You are highly favored. The Lord is with you."

Do you really know this? Do you understand it in your soul? When fear is gripping your mind, when the phone rings at 3 a.m., when the doctor looks worried, when the news comes that changes how you see the world, do you realize you are still blessed and highly favored? Do you realize that God hasn't gone anywhere? He's still right there with you. God said He will never leave you nor forsake you (Deuteronomy 31:6).

You were blessed yesterday when you had good news, and you are still blessed today with this new news. I say "new news" because God can make bad news good. Nothing is impossible for God. We have a tendency to see things from only one perspective, but God sees things from His divine perspective. We might think something is bad, but it turns out to be exactly what we need. Once we fasten our faith in the assurance of God's presence, knowing that He is with us and that we are blessed no matter what, we can begin to move away from our fear and into faith.

Gabriel told Mary, "Rejoice!" In other words, he said go ahead and change your spiritual disposition. You may not understand it or feel comfortable with it, but rejoice. I understand you have a lot of questions; you're nervous and maybe a little worried, but rejoice because God is with you. Mary had to deal with whether Joseph would stay with her and whether her mother and father would believe her. She had to deal with whether society would marginalize her or make her an outcast.

In order for her to deal with these things, Mary first had to understand in her soul that God was with her. That's important for us to remember. Because to deal with the fear in your life, you have to be like David and say, "Though I walk through the valley of the shadow of death, I will fear no evil" (Psalm 23:4). Why? Because God is with me. We can cope with the realities of life when we first fasten our faith to the assurance of God's presence with a positive praise disposition.

Second, we can follow Mary's example and fasten our faith to the acceptance of God's plan. This can be found in Luke 1:29-33. Gabriel laid out the entire scenario to tell Mary that God clearly had a plan for her and her baby. Mary didn't understand all these details. You can imagine her wondering, "What do you mean He's going to overshadow me?" She didn't know what Gabriel was talking about, but Gabriel said God had it planned; and so that, after some time thinking about it, was fine with Mary. She may have been stunned by the initial encounter, but after thinking about it, she decided to accept God's plan and purpose based on faith.

That's true for our lives as well. We don't always understand why God allows some things to happen, but we have to trust and believe everything is part of His plan. If He allows it, and since we know He is always with us, we have to trust Him and His plans. Mary had her doubts. We see that when she asked, "How can this be?" But after thinking about it for some time, she decided to trust God's plan—and so can we.

Sometimes we get caught up wondering how something is going to work out, so we might even be tempted to hold on to fear. At some point, if you want to get past your fear, you have to make up your mind that God is God and you are the servant. That's what Mary did. "Behold, the handmaid of the Lord." Okay, God, You're the boss. As You wish. If You say so. You got it.

Of course, when we face fear in our lives, we wrestle with questions. *How God? How are You going to bring me out of this? How are You going to open the door? How are You going to make a way?* What we need to do is rearrange the three letters of "how" and instead begin asking "Who?" This is the third lesson we learn from Mary in verses 34, 35, and 37.

We need to fasten our faith to the assistance of God's power. We don't have to spend our time worrying about the *how*, we need to focus our mind on the *who*. That was Mary's eventual conclusion: "I don't know how overshadowing gets me pregnant, but I know who said it would work. I don't understand how this baby is going to become the King of kings, but I know who does." (In fact, she still didn't understand it thirty-three years later when Jesus was hanging on the cross; but three days after the crucifixion, on Resurrection Sunday, it became a lot clearer for her.)

I'm not saying this is easy to do. It wasn't easy for Mary. She was not exceptional; she was just like us. She struggled with her faith—many the people in the Bible did—but she trusted and made the right decisions. Even while she was still a bit doubtful, yet beginning to believe, she remembered what Gabriel said about her cousin Elizabeth being pregnant. After some time thinking, Mary visited her cousin. No sooner than Mary called her name, Elizabeth started praising God, confirming everything Gabriel had told her.

Sometimes when we're stuck on the *how*, we need to witness God's power as it manifests in the lives of other believers to help us get over the hump of fear and doubt. That's part of the power of corporate worship: being able to rub shoulders with other people who can witness to you about God's power to do what He says He's going to do, even when it seems impossible. Mary's visit to her cousin proved to be the very thing she needed to seal her decision to trust and move fully past her fear.

The fourth lesson we learn is to fasten our faith on the acceptance of God's promises and purpose. Mary moved past her doubt and fear after her visit with Elizabeth confirmed the wonder working power of God. What was impossible in Mary's mind was manifested in the pregnancy of her cousin. So then, what she struggled to believe became real for her. She believed it fully and trusted completely that God's promise and His purpose would come to pass. She finally did exactly what Gabriel told her to do at the beginning of the encounter: she rejoiced.

Perhaps you have heard the expression, "God said it. I believe it. That settles it." A better expression, however, is "God said it. That settles it. Hallelujah!" Once you come to this state of faith, you have no option but to rejoice. Mary said, "My soul doth magnify the Lord" (verse 46). In fact, she got her praise going for real. "And my spirit hath rejoiced in God my Saviour. For he hath regarded the low estate of his handmaiden: for, behold, from henceforth all generations shall call me blessed. For he that is mighty hath done to me great things; and holy is his name. And his mercy is on them that fear him from generation to generation. He hath shewed strength with his arm; he hath scattered the proud in the imagination of their hearts. He hath put down the mighty from their seats, and exalted them of low degree. He hath filled the hungry with good things; and the rich he hath sent empty away" (verses 47-53).

Reflect for a moment on what Mary had declared. Where did all of this come from?

Gabriel didn't say all that, did he? We don't see that in the text, but we can determine that she had apparently anchored her faith firmly in the power and character of God whereby she is now giving expression of her vibrant faith. Her mind and perspective about herself changed. This declaration is her personal testimony of struggle. She was lowly in her own eyes, and now she has been made great. She realized what Gabriel told her was true: She *was* highly favored. Her family feared and honored God for generations and was now being honored for it. These are Mary's own declarations based on her faith and belief that have replaced her fear. She accepted God's promises and purpose and overcome the frightening flip bag of fear.

> KEEP THE FEAR SMALL RATHER THAN ALLOW IT TO BECOME A HUGE CUMBERSOME BAG YOU TOTE AROUND.

Finally, Mary's song of praise in verses 46-56 teaches us to fasten our faith to the allegiance of God's praise. Praise strengthens and reinforces our faith. It is our continual praise that helps us maintain our victory over fear.

It's normal to have a little fear. That's the idea of the flip bag. Yes, you can tuck it away, but it's still there. The key is to keep it little and not let it open up and begin to grab hold to everything you have. Keep the fear small rather than allow it to become a huge cumbersome bag you tote around. Keep it fastened up by remembering Mary and Gabriel and the lessons of their encounter. When human beings come in touch with the supernatural—when God calls us in our lives, challenges us, changes our plans and goals—it can be scary. But knowing God is with us is the first step toward faith and fastening up the frightening flip bag of fear.

> KNOWING GOD IS WITH US IS THE FIRST STEP TOWARD FAITH AND FASTENING UP THE FRIGHTENING FLIP BAG OF FEAR.

CHAPTER 8
The Bulging Backpack of Bitterness

"Looking carefully lest anyone fall short of the grace of God;
lest any root of bitterness springing up cause trouble, and by this
many become defiled."
(Hebrews 12:15, NKJV)

There is a story about a man who was bitten by a dog. As a result of the bite, he developed rabies and had to be taken to the hospital. Unfortunately, at the time there was no treatment available to cure rabies. The doctor had to give this bad news to the patient.

"Sir," the doctor said, "I am sorry to tell you that we've done all we can do. Unfortunately, there is no treatment for your condition. The best I can do is to try to make you comfortable. I don't want to give you any false hope. My advice to you is to get your affairs in order as soon as possible."

The dying man was shocked and began to settle into depression.

After a moment, he suddenly perked up and asked the doctor if he might have a pen and a piece of paper. The doctor obliged, and the man began writing.

Hours later, the doctor returned to check on his patient and found he was still diligently writing away on the paper. Encouraged by his good attitude, the doctor said, "I'm happy to see that you took my advice to write out your will."

The man turned to the doctor and said, "No, doc, I'm not working on my will. I'm making a list of people I'd like to see before I die."

The doctor was impressed. "Ah, so you can tell them what they mean to you?" he asked.

"No," the man said, "so I can bite them."

137

BITTEN WITH POISON

This story conveys the idea of the bulging backpack of bitterness. Bitterness is like being bitten, then biting others in return. In fact, the word *bitterness* comes from the root word *biter*, which means "to be bitten." Unfortunately, we all know what it's like to be bitten, to have hard feelings over something that's been done to us. If we have not experienced bitterness ourselves, certainly we know someone who has. The strange thing about bitterness is that, like a backpack, we can't always see that we're carrying it. Other people can see it hanging on our backs, but unless we pay close attention, we might fail to notice that bitterness is weighing us down.

> BITTERNESS IS LIKE BEING BITTEN, THEN BITING OTHERS IN RETURN.

I've seen people get saddled with the backpack of bitterness in many unexpected ways. Some were fired from their jobs for an unfair or false reason. Others committed their lives to love until death do them part, but their partners walked out on them without a second glance. Some felt it's their duty to help friends or loved ones in times of need, even at great sacrifice to themselves; but when they found themselves in need, their friends and loved ones did not answer their phones. They got bit and became bitter.

Some had someone they trusted say something horrible about them, betray their trust, or reveal their secrets; and they found themselves with a backpack of bitterness. For some, it goes back even further to when they were abandoned by a mother; abused by a father; or rejected as a child and, as a result, they have stayed bitter for years—possibly decades.

Bitterness makes us sour and angry. Like being bitten by a serpent, it contaminates our spirits with poisonous venom that eats at us like a cancer until it leaves us as empty and useless as a rusty can. In fact, of all the emotional baggage I've discussed so far, none is more debilitating than bitterness. Bitterness is like Satan himself injecting all the poison of hell directly into your veins. In fact, Peter, in Acts 8:23, said to Simon, "I perceive that thou art in the gall of bitterness." The word *gall* in this instance actually means "poison."

No doubt this is the reason the Holy Spirit says in Hebrews 12:15 that we need to be diligent about ensuring no root of bitterness springs up in our lives. How do we do that? How can we ensure we don't end up saddled with the bulging backpack of bitterness, with its poison leeching into us?

To guard against bitterness, we have to discover where bitterness comes from. There are three common causes of bitterness that Jesus discusses in the Sermon on the Mount that will help us recognize how bitterness comes to us. This list is not an exhaustive list.

THREE CAUSES OF BITTERNESS

The first cause of bitterness mentioned in the Bible is found in the words of Jesus in Matthew 5:11-12. Here Jesus says, "Blessed are ye, when men shall revile you, and persecute you, and shall say all manner of evil against you falsely, for my sake. Rejoice, and be exceeding glad: for great is your reward in heaven: for so persecuted they the prophets which were before you." The first source of bitterness is what is said about us.

If you are like most people, you know what it is like to have someone say something evil or erroneous about you. Jesus calls it "all manner of evil against you falsely" (Matthew 5:11). It is a horrible feeling. Few things hurt us more than having our good intentions maligned or having someone criticize, defame, or humiliate us.

In this verse, Jesus tells us how to avoid bitterness when people say wrong things about us. Rather than becoming upset and allowing the poison of someone's words to seep into our souls, we should, instead, rejoice because that is exactly how people treated the prophets and the Lord Himself. Of course, the prophets and the Lord experienced acute persecution for their righteous stance, which often resulted in martyrdom. Conversely, the form of persecution we experience in the Western world pales in comparison. However, we are expected to respond as prescribed by Christ with an attitude, whereby we rejoice as opposed to seeking revenge.

The apostle Paul concurs that our response to evil is never that of evil. He explains in Romans 12:17-21 how we are to respond: "Recompense to no man evil for evil. Provide things honest in the sight of all men. If it be possible, as much as lieth in you, live peaceably with all men. Dearly beloved, avenge not yourselves, but rather give place unto wrath: for it is written, Vengence is mine; I will repay, saith the Lord. Therefore, if thine enemy hunger, feed him; if he thirst, give him drink; for in so doing, thou shalt heap coals of fire on his head. Be not overcome of evil, but overcome evil with good."

In other words, if people are talking negatively about you, you are in good company. They did it to Jesus and to all of God's representatives. Rather than looking at it as a negative thing, look at it as evidence that you are on the right path. If they talked about Christ, they are certainly going to talk about you. Jesus says that we receive a great reward when we endure such persecution. So rather than becoming bitter, rejoice!

The second cause of bitterness comes as a result of what is done to us. In Matthew 5:38-39 Jesus says, "Ye have heard that it hath been said, An eye for an eye, and a tooth for a tooth: But I say unto you, That ye resist not evil: but whosoever shall smite thee on thy right cheek, turn to him the other also."

Jesus is explaining that it is not what happens to us that matters to God; it is how we respond to it. Your spouse may decide to leave you after many years of marriage, and you may be tempted to be bitter. How do you respond to what has been done to you? Some people are so bitter that they use their innocent children to try to hurt their ex-spouses. They usually don't realize how hurtful, insensitive, and cruel they are being—not to the spouse but to the children. Jesus says it's not about paying someone back for the evil they've done to you; Jesus will deal with them. Instead, let it go. As a child of God, you are going to be fine. Let it go. Let it roll off your back; don't store it in your bulging backpack.

The third cause of bitterness is what is taken from us. Verse 40 says, "And if any man will sue thee at the law, and take away thy coat, let him have thy cloak also." Jesus says it is better to be wronged than to do wrong. When someone wrongs you (and someone will sooner or later), you have one of two choices: you can either get bitter, or you can be bigger.

As a child of God, understand that God is in the business of restoration. Whatever someone takes from you, God is more than able to restore it to you. The broken heart that someone trampled, God can restore it with new love. You lost a house in the financial crisis; you can get a new one. Whatever you feel you have lost, God is able to restore it and make it better than it was before. Trust Him, and know this is true.

When someone wrongs you, you can be bigger by not retaliating. After all, when you retaliate, you're acting small, not big, not better. You're acting as if whatever you lost was as good as it gets. It's not. It can get a lot better. God can show you if you trust Him. If they take it away, let it go. Expect something better. It's as if God is cleaning out your closet and making room for something new and better. When you get mad about what you lost, it means you don't believe there's something more out there or something better coming that God desires for you. Let God make room by trusting in His provision and care. He is in the restoration business.

We get bitter one of three ways: Someone said something to us; someone did something to us; or someone took something from us.

THE CONSEQUENCES OF BITTERNESS

What happens when you decide to ignore what Jesus says and accept the poison of bitterness running through your body? If we go back to Hebrews 12, we see the writer uses a poignant word picture of a weed growing in a garden to illustrate the consequences of bitterness: "Lest any *root* of bitterness springing up trouble you" (verse 15, italics added).

If you know anything about weeds, you learn quickly that it doesn't help to cut them. In fact, most weeds have such delicate seed hoods that if the plant gets even as much as shaken, it sets loose the seeds that spread it.

Consider the common dandelion. They have those pretty yellow flowers at first, but soon afterward those ugly, white cotton-like seed hoods shoot up. All it takes is a gentle breeze to send those dandelion seeds flying all over the neighborhood. Although they fly gently, when they land, they hold fast and quickly take root. If you cut weeds while they are in your yard, it will look fine for a day or so. You won't even notice them; but then they grow much quicker than grass, and in a couple of days you'll soon see a yard full of weeds. Weeds shouldn't be cut. To get rid of weeds, you must pluck them out, root and all.

The writer of Hebrews says to uproot bitterness before it takes over our lives. The word *trouble* in verse 12 is sometimes translated as "vex." The idea is that bitterness, like a weed, can grow so fast and strong that it soon starts to dominate you mentally. You may be like a freshly mowed lawn: You look good today, but when you allow bitterness to dwell in your heart (as soon as you see that person who did you wrong or as soon as you start thinking about what so-and-so did to you), you become consumed by it. You see, there is no passion in the human heart that promises as much yet pays so little. The more you let bitterness grow, the more it takes over the soil of your heart.

In the Southern United States where I live, there is a plant called kudzu. It can grow one foot in a single day and one hundred feet in a single growing season. It has come to be called "The Plant That Ate the South" due to the fact that it clings to buildings, chokes out other plants, and takes over everything in its path if it is not controlled.

This is how bitterness works in your life. If you have bitterness, your mind gets constantly drawn to the people you are bitter toward. You can't stop thinking about them. They take up mental residence in your life and vex you. When you become bitter, you allow a person to rent space in your mind for free. You can't enjoy life because you're so bitter against that person, and all you can do is plot to get even or retaliate.

The second consequence of bitterness is that it will depress you emotionally. Bitterness is a depressant. If you pay attention to bitter people, you will notice that none of them are happy. There are no happy, bitter people. Bitter people are critical, cynical, negative, pessimistic, and distracted. They are marked with a spirit of depression. You could be having a good day and have lunch with a bitter person and, suddenly, you're having a bad day, too. Why? Because bitterness can be contagious. It can be a barricade to your joy, peace, happiness, and sense of security. Bitterness will impair your functionality. You can't live peaceably with bitterness; it needs to be uprooted and burned in the fire of forgiveness.

Another horrible consequence of bitterness is that it will debilitate you physically. More than fifty diseases, ranging from ulcers to high blood pressure, can be caused by bitterness. Of course, that doesn't mean every sick person is bitter or that every bitter person is sick. What it does mean is that every person who remains bitter will somehow be affected physically by bitterness. Eventually, bitterness will give you health challenges if you keep holding on to it.

Even though bitter people spend much of their time plotting how they are going to hurt someone else, in reality, the bitter person hurts no one more than himself or herself. Bitterness does much more damage to the vessel in which it is *stored* than to the person on whom it is *poured*.

Bitterness will also disconnect you relationally. The reason for this isn't hard to understand. Like all the other types of emotional baggage we've discussed thus far can hinder your relationship with God and with others, so can bitterness. If you allow bitterness to reign in your life, you will find yourself alone because no one wants to be around mean, bitter people. If you find people leaving out the back door whenever you come in the front door or avoiding you and cutting conversations short, perhaps you should look behind you to see if you've got a bulging backpack of bitterness hanging on you.

Finally, bitterness will damage you spiritually. Hebrews says, "Looking diligently lest any man fail of the grace of God" (12:15). What does that mean? It doesn't mean God's grace fails; it means we fail to take advantage of His grace. This is exactly what the bitter believer does. He has a grace deficiency. If he accepts the fact that he has been forgiven (graced), he should be able to extend similar grace to the one who has offended him. Instead, bitter people tend to focus on the negative all of the time. They not only fail to see the grace of God at work in own their lives, but they also fail to see any good in anything or anyone else. That's how bitterness can damage and destroy you spiritually.

Bitterness can also get in the way of your worship because it is hard, if not impossible, to pray and worship when your mind is constantly focused on negative stuff as a result of an unresolved offense harbored in your heart against another person. It is for this reason that Jesus states in a very stern fashion Matthew 5:23-24: "Therefore if thou bring thy gift to the altar, and there rememberest that thy brother hath ought against thee; leave there thy gift before the altar, and go thy way; first be reconciled to thy brother, and then come and offer thy gift."

Bitterness will weaken your witness and taint your testimony. It will seal the lips of a soul winner. Bitterness will also affect your capacity to receive the Word. Remember when Jesus taught about the seed falling on good soil? If you allow bitterness to take root in your heart, there is no good soil for God's Word to fall on. All the good soil is full of weeds. The seed of God's Word can't be sown in your life.

Furthermore, a bitter person isn't trying to hear God's Word. Have you heard the expression, "I ain't trying to hear that"? It came out in the 80's or 90's. Someone would ask, "Do you hear what I'm saying?" and the other person would reply, "I ain't trying to hear that." It means, "I don't care about what you're saying."

What you're saying is unimportant or irrelevant. That's how the bitter person looks at God's Word.

The bitter person is only thinking about the thing, the person, the issue, or the situation that occupies his or her mind. Bitter people aren't trying to hear Jesus talk about forgiveness or loving your enemies. They aren't trying to hear God at all. Bitterness is a poison far too risky to allow in our bodies.

THE BITTERNESS CURE

So then how do we cure bitterness?

The first step is to pursue peace. Hebrew 12:14 says, "Follow peace with all men and holiness, without which no man shall see the Lord." Notice the writer doesn't say pursue peace with people you like. Also notice he doesn't say wait around and let other people pursue peace with you. That's what a lot of bitter people do. They sit around waiting for someone to apologize to them. No, that's not what the writer of Hebrews says here. He says we are to be the ones who pursue peace.

You know what *pursue* means? Think of where you hear this word used most. Someone who's unemployed might pursue a job. They want a job, need a job, so they do what they have to do to get one. On the news, you will hear about a high-speed pursuit—the police pursuing a suspect, a criminal. That's the same energy we should have when we pursue peace with those who have offended us. Don't wait for them to come to you. Pursue peace because you're the bigger person. You're the mature one, the child of God. To this end, Jesus says in the Beatitudes, "Blessed are the peacemakers: for they shall be called the children of God" (Matthew 5:9). If you have someone you have some bitterness toward, go to him or her so you can have peace.

Pursuing peace means doing what is right so you can be right with God. It does not mean you need to be bosom buddies with the person who wronged you. There's a difference between our obligation to forgive and our option to reconcile. You can forgive independently. You don't need the other person to do anything for you in order to forgive; but if you're going to be reconciled, that requires the other person's collaboration. Amos 3:3 says, "Can two walk together, except they be agreed?" Certainly, the Lord expects us to forgive with the desire to reconcile. If we can reconcile, it is good to do so, but sometimes it is better to be at peace and apart.

The second cure for bitterness is to place it in the past. You can't continue to allow historical events to affect your future. At some point, you have to decide to leave the past in the past. That's why the rearview mirror is smaller than the windshield in your car. You can glance in the past, but you must focus on what's ahead of you.

Paul says in Ephesians 4:31, "Let all bitterness, and wrath, and anger, and clamour, and evil speaking, be put away from you, with all malice." The words *put away* mean "dispose of" or "discard." Get rid of bitterness. If you're going to get the bulging backpack of bitterness off your back, you have to remove the "get even" feeling out of your heart. Bury the problem in an unmarked grave so you won't be able to go back, find it, and dig it up again.

When you're bitter, you carry the person you are bitter toward on your back in that backpack. If you're bitter at your boss, it's as if you're carrying your boss right on your back. If you're angry with your mother-in-law, she's in that backpack as well. How many people can you carry on your back? Can you imagine how much easier it will be to walk if you let them all go?

The final cure for bitterness is to pass on pardon. In the next verse in Ephesians, Paul says, "And be ye kind one to another, tenderhearted, forgiving one another, even as God for Christ's sake hath forgiven you" (verse 32). Notice that term "tenderhearted." Bitterness and unforgiveness cause spiritual sclerosis, the hardening of our hearts. Forgiveness, however, softens it.

We are motivated to forgive others as God has forgiven us. It doesn't matter what kind of wrong another person has done to you. No matter how much has been done to you, it is not as much as was done to Jesus on the cross. No one has ever been treated as awful as our Lord. Even as He was dying on the cross for our sins,

He said, "Father, forgive them; for they know not what they do" (Luke 23:34).

The great preacher and theologian Charles Spurgeon said, "Let us go to Calvary to learn how we may be forgiven, and then let us linger there to learn how to forgive—forgive freely, forgive fully, and forgive finally."[9]

If you need to forgive someone who has wronged you, you must forgive that person freely. Whether he asks for it or not—and forgive fully. Uproot all the bitterness within you, once and for all.

I didn't say it would be easy. Many people have taken their bitterness with them to the grave, but that's not the way God wants us to live. He wants us to know the fullness of living in forgiveness. Not only His forgiveness, but also the freedom we have when we forgive others as we have been forgiven. It truly makes no sense to keep holding on to stuff from the past. You have an entire life to live and no time to waste. Let it go and move on.

> WE WASTE SO MUCH OF THE PRECIOUS COMMODITY OF LIFE AND JOY BY CARRYING AROUND THE BULGING BACKPACK OF BITTERNESS FULL OF MEMORIES AND PEOPLE WHO HAVE HURT US, EMBARRASSED US, ABUSED US, USED US, LIED TO US, CHEATED ON US, STOLEN FROM US, AND HURT US.

A wise man stood before an audience and told a funny joke. The entire room erupted in laughter and screams of delight. He continued with another interesting story, and then repeated the same joke again. Upon hearing it the second time, fewer people laughed. He went on with other stories, delighting the audience, but then told the same joke a third time. Almost no one laughed. During the course of his speech, he told the same joke three more times. By the last telling, no one laughed. The wise man then smiled and said, "You can't laugh at the same joke again and again, so why do you keep crying over the same things again and again?"

There's a lot of wisdom in that story. We waste so much of the precious commodity of life and joy by carrying around the bulging backpack of bitterness full of memories and people who have hurt us, embarrassed us, abused us, used us, lied to us, cheated on us, stolen from us, and hurt us. Carrying them around doesn't stop the pain. Plotting revenge doesn't stop the pain. Wishing them ill doesn't stop the pain. The only thing that stops the pain and torment is forgiveness. By forgiving, we can finally be free of this nagging, distracting, and health-stealing weight and walk in the power and joy that God intended for us.

> BY FORGIVING, WE CAN FINALLY BE FREE OF THIS NAGGING, DISTRACTING, AND HEALTH-STEALING WEIGHT AND WALK IN THE POWER AND JOY THAT GOD INTENDED FOR US.

CHAPTER 9
The Ugly Utility Bag of Unforgiveness

"Peter came to him and asked, 'Lord, how often should I forgive someone who sins against me? Seven times?' 'No, not seven times,' Jesus replied, 'but seventy times seven!'"
(Matthew 18:21-22, NLT)

Congratulations! We have come to the final chapter; and, by now, if you've implemented these teachings, you feel much lighter on your journey. You should have both the knowledge and the confidence that life does not need to be burdensome.

Together, we've studied how to get rid of a number of cumbersome, heavy, and irritating bags that cause so many people to slow down, fall behind, and exhaust themselves—bags God never intended us to carry. Good riddance!

We have . . .

- ditched the Draining Duffle Bag of Depression, Doubt, and Defeatism,
- abandoned the Agonizing Attaché Case of Anxiety,
- heaved off the Heavy Handbag of Hopelessness and Discouragement,
- gotten rid of the Grievous Grip of Guilt,
- pitched the Problematic Pouch of People-Pleasing,
- left the Loathsome Luggage of Low Self-Esteem,
- forsaken the Frightening Flip Bag of Fear, and
- banished the Bulging Backpack of Bitterness.

Now we've come to the final bag and the longest chapter. It's time for us to unload the Ugly Utility Bag of Unforgiveness.

I saved this bag for last because for many it is the hardest bag to release. If you began this chapter directly after reading the last chapter, you may recognize some connections herein. Although I tell people how to get rid of bitterness through forgiveness, many people still struggle with it. That's why we need this chapter. We need to talk about that stubborn need to hold on to unforgiveness.

REASONS FOR UNFORGIVENESS

So many of us struggle with unforgiveness. The reasons vary. Some feel forgiving wrongs that have been done to us leaves us open to having them repeated. For instance, if you forgive someone who lied to you, cheated on you, or stole from you, they may well do it again. Honestly, that *could* happen.

For others, it may be the feeling that you have not experienced forgiveness yourself that makes you hold on to a wrong. For someone who may have fallen on hard times at some point in his life and, perhaps, messed up his credit, we know that the credit bureau makes sure everyone he does business with knows about it. The credit bureaus don't seem to forgive or forget. The same can be true at our jobs. Our performance records may be referred to often in evaluations, a constant reminder of our shortcomings or successes, whichever they may be. Maybe the fact that other people don't forget your mistakes makes you feel justified in holding on to theirs.

Still, there can be much deeper and more painful reasons for not forgiving someone. You've been hurt; someone you love has been hurt; or you have lost something valuable, and you want recompense. Can you blame the relatives of a murder victim for holding on to their anger and unforgiveness? Can you blame the victim of a rape for being unwilling to forgive her rapist or the victim of child or domestic abuse her abuser? Sometimes the grieving isn't done yet. There's too much pain. Psychologists say that the process of crawling out of the pit of pain can be harder to deal with than the tragedy that originally landed some in that pit. For many, forgiving the person who murdered their loved one feels like betraying their loved one.

On the other hand, sometimes the person you are trying to forgive keeps hurting you. Perhaps this person has a drug addiction or is plain evil and gets pleasure from causing you pain. There is such a thing as toxic people, which we have previously discussed. You may forgive again and again, only to have that person hurt you, or try to hurt you, again and again. People often think forgiveness means tolerating someone's hurtful behavior. They may want or need the person who offended them to ask forgiveness before they can give it. In most cases, the person who caused the offense has gone on their merry way with nary a second thought about the one hurt or offended.

There are also people who believe forgiving someone means not seeking justice for the wrong. You may want justice, but seeking forgiveness feels like betraying that desire for righteousness to prevail. Others did not grow up in a home where they saw authentic forgiveness practiced. They may have had to jump through hoops to be forgiven, and they expect others to do the same thing. Some people even need to use their anger to comfort their pain.

These reasons tend to be more noble reasons for not extending forgiveness. Not all the reasons are so noble. Sometimes we fail to forgive others because we don't value our relationship with them. We don't care about them, and we don't feel we need them in our lives, so good riddance. Peace. See ya. Hasta la vista. It doesn't matter if they want forgiveness or not, and we may not care enough about them to bother finding out. We don't think we need the person, so we have no tolerance for their behavior.

For some, pride or ego is to blame. The other person is simply unworthy of forgiveness. The offenders haven't prostrated themselves enough, fallen face down, and begged. They don't look sorry enough. These people may not see their sins as forgiven or understand their need to forgive others as they have been forgiven. They spend too much time focused on the "enemy" rather than on God and His Word. These people misunderstand the damage unforgiveness does to their own hearts.

SOME PEOPLE THINK FORGIVENESS MAKES THEM LOOK WEAK, STUPID, OR NAÏVE.

Other people don't forgive because they want to use their anger as leverage to control other people. They identify themselves as victims and use that fact to get what they want or need from others. Some want the other party to make the first move, and some people think forgiveness makes them look weak, stupid, or naïve.

If you struggle with forgiveness because you have experienced deep hurt that has left you debilitated and unable to imagine forgiving someone, I want you to read this chapter, but I also recognize that you may be in need of professional Christian grief counseling. As with those who are seriously depressed, I want you to be willing to seek the help of a professional counselor who can help you work through the emotional and mental barriers blocking your forgiveness. I don't want to add to your pain by making you feel guilty for something you are unable at this moment to do alone. There are already too many people in the world who are alienated by family members and churches because of their inability to forgive someone who has hurt them.

If you are the victim of serious emotional trauma, I encourage you to work through those issues with a trained professional. As I mentioned in the chapter on depression, there is nothing wrong with that, and you should have no qualms about seeking the help you need psychologically or spiritually any more than someone who wears glasses seeks help for their vision. God has given men and women wisdom to help us deal with the many mental and emotional challenges we face in life. If we need these means of help and remedies, we should use them without fear or shame.

MOVING PAST OUR PAINS

For most people, holding onto unforgiveness isn't about suffering serious emotional trauma. Rather, it's about learning to look at our situation as God sees it in order to move past our pain and focus on Christ. Thankfully, most people have not been victimized by serious emotional trauma, such as murder. Realizing there are people who suffer from such horrible pain may help many of us move closer to extending forgiveness to those who have offended us.

If there is one thing that has become clear throughout my life, it is that "to live is to forgive." Life constantly presents offenses to us; we must learn to forgive. This is regardless of whether the person who offended us apologizes or makes recompense. The road to healing and freedom is paved with forgiveness. If we do not forgive, we bind ourselves to the past. In fact, there is room in the utility bag of unforgiveness for a number of other bags—guilt, depression, bitterness, anger, hopelessness, pain, and regret. So in order to gain our own freedom, we must forgive!

"TO LIVE IS TO FORGIVE"

Apart from the reason I listed above, many times we resist forgiving because we misunderstand it. To clear up the record and clarify what I mean by forgiveness, it is easier to discuss what forgiveness is *not* rather than what it is. Forgiveness does not mean:

1. Approving of what someone else did
2. Pretending the offense never took place
3. Overlooking abuse
4. Making excuses for other people's bad behavior
5. Justifying evil
6. Denying that others have hurt you (perhaps repeatedly)
7. Letting others walk all over you or use you
8. Refusing to press charges or call the police when a crime or abuse has been committed
9. Forgetting the crime that was done
10. Pretending you were never hurt
11. Restoring the relationship to what it was before
12. Being bosom buddies again
13. Having total reconciliation
14. Cancelling out the negative consequences of sin

That's a long list, but it's helpful to clear up misconceptions about the meaning of forgiveness before we get further into this chapter. If you were thinking that in order to forgive one of these fourteen things had to happen, it isn't true. These things may happen, but they are not what forgiveness means.

So then what is forgiveness?

Christian psychologist Archibald Hart says *forgiveness* is "surrendering my right to hurt you for hurting me."[10] I like that definition because it fits most situations well. When we've been offended, we want to get that person back. Forgiveness is giving up that right and releasing that intent to get even.

Some people don't believe forgiveness is necessary because they may have heard it said that "time heals all wounds"; but I can tell you that time does not heal anything when it comes to forgiveness. We can ignore an injury, but we cannot pretend the pain that resulted does not exist. When someone offends or wrongs us, we need to deal with it God's way, and we should deal with it quickly. Jesus said if you have something against someone, you shouldn't even make your offering to God until you first resolve that issue (Matthew 5:23-24). That's how serious God is about forgiveness. Why? Because unforgiveness is a dangerous poison.

ALLOWING POISON TO FESTER

There is a story of two friends, Shawn and Mark, who got into an argument as they walked down the street. Shawn got so angry that he shoved Mark to the ground. When Mark fell, he landed on a nail, which went through his pants and into his leg. Shawn apologized and tried to help Mark up to remove the nail and treat his wound, but Mark refused his help. In fact, Mark said he intended to leave the nail right where it was to serve as a constant reminder to both of them of how cruel and mean Shawn had been to him. You can guess the rest of the story. Infection eventually set in, and Mark eventually died.

We look at a story like that and laugh at how ridiculous Mark behaved in that situation. Who would leave a rusty nail in his leg just for spite? Yet, if you think about it, that is exactly what we do when we refuse to forgive. We allow a poison to fester in our bodies. Shawn may or may not have felt bad about Mark deciding to leave that nail in his leg. For all we know, Shawn went on with his life and never thought about Mark again, or maybe Shawn was racked with guilt the rest of his life; but that is the point—it doesn't matter what Shawn did. Mark is the one who had to forgive in order to be healed. If we allow unforgiveness to remain in our hearts, it can kill us. That's why Jesus says to act quickly to forgive. Unforgiveness can ruin our relationships, crush our spirits, and hinder our walk with God.

Furthermore, it's important to understand, as believers, that forgiveness is not optional; it is obligatory. It is part and parcel of our identity in Christ. In Matthew 6:14, Jesus says it directly: "For if you forgive other people when they sin against you, your heavenly Father will also forgive you" (NIV). We have been forgiven, and we are commanded to forgive—unlimitedly and even when undeserved.

The best metaphor I can think of to help explain forgiveness is a funeral. At every funeral, friends and family grieve their loss, but then there is the moment when they must leave it behind. When they are at the cemetery, no matter how much pain they feel or how long they linger at the grave, there comes a time when they must get into their cars and leave. They can't stay there. They have to go. They have to leave the loss behind, buried deep in the ground.

The same is true of forgiveness. You can grieve what happened to you, but you have to let it go, or it will damage you. As uncomfortable as it may be to read and hear, at some point, you have to bury it.

Jesus told the powerful story of the unforgiving debtor in Matthew 18:21-35. It is one of the most dramatic and stunning stories Jesus tells in the Bible. The story begins with Peter making an inquisition of Jesus. He wanted to know the answer to a question that's been bugging him related to something Jesus taught earlier in the chapter. Jesus had finished teaching his followers how to deal with someone who sins against another believer. Jesus said to go to the person privately and deal with it. If the person doesn't listen, take two witnesses with you from the church and try again. If the person doesn't listen to the church's decision, treat them as an unbeliever. This teaching triggered something for Peter.

It seems pretty clear that Peter perhaps had someone in mind when he asked this question of Jesus. He wanted Jesus to help him with a personal matter: "Lord, how often should I forgive someone who sins against me? Seven times?" (Matthew 18:21, NLT).

What's interesting about Peter's inquisition is he already had the answer. It's like he was trying to help Jesus out. The rabbis had taught that Jews were supposed to forgive someone three times. Peter had been around Jesus long enough to figure Jesus would have a higher standard, so he doubled the number the rabbis used and added one more. Peter indicated to Jesus that someone had been testing his faith and he was willing to hold out for at least seven times, but that's where he drew the line. Peter thought he was being good and righteous. He thought he could impress Jesus and force Him to set a limit on the number of times he had to forgive someone.

Jesus, however, surprised Peter with his injunction, his command. Jesus said, "Well, Peter, you're on the right track, but not seven times. No, you should forgive seventy times seven times."

Now I imagine you might be thinking like Peter was: What's seventy times seven? Mmm, zero, seven times seven—forty-nine—490? You would need to carry a notebook with you to write down all the times the person sinned against you to make sure you didn't accidentally pay them back on the 487th time.

That's not what Jesus means. He doesn't want you to track the number of times someone sins against you. The point is that He wants you to develop a habit of forgiveness; He wants you to forgive an infinite number of times. He wants forgiveness to become second nature to you, your automatic response. If someone sins against you, you forgive him or her. That's it. The offense should not linger. You should not track it. You should not hold onto it. Jesus said if they strike you on one cheek, offer them the other. If they make you carry their stuff one mile, offer to carry it two. Let forgiveness reign in your heart and mind. Be a forgiving person. Don't waste any time with someone's offense; forgive it.

Jesus illustrated what the kingdom of heaven is like in verse 23. Whenever Jesus used the term "kingdom of heaven," He was giving a peek into the supernatural realm, showing us how God sees things. In this illustration, Jesus told of a king who was owed a great debt by one of his servants. The amount of the debt in today's dollars would be about $25 million dollars. The king had his accountants square up his books. The indebted servant was brought before him, but he could not repay the debt. The king then ordered the servant, his wife, his children, and everything he owned to be sold to pay the debt. Jesus says the indebted servant fell on his knees and begged the king, "Please be patient with me, and I will repay it all." Jesus said the king felt pity, released him, and forgave his entire debt.

The servant simply asked for more time, but the king knew there was no way the man could ever repay the debt in his lifetime. You have to wonder what the servant did with all the money he borrowed, but it doesn't matter. The point of the story is that the servant didn't have it, and the king forgave the debt. Can you imagine owing millions of dollars and the debt is forgiven? I know a lot of people who would be happy if they could have their student loans forgiven. Imagine if the bank forgave your mortgage, your car loan, and your credit card bills. That's not just good news, that's great news! I'll even venture to say it was the best news that servant ever had his whole life. I imagine he was as happy as he could be when he left the king.

But that's not the end of the story.

The servant, after leaving the king, went to a fellow servant who owed him a few thousand dollars. Not a million. Not hundreds of thousands. This same servant, who had just been forgiven $25 *million* dollars, went to a fellow servant—another guy exactly like him—

—who owed him a few thousand dollars. The servant grabbed the man by the throat and demanded instant payment. This man did the same thing the original servant had done before the king: He fell on his knees and begged for more time with the exact plea. He had a much greater chance of being able to come up with the few thousand than the original servant had of coming up with millions. But instead of being merciful, as the king had been with him, the servant had his fellow servant arrested and put in prison until the debt could be paid in full.

In other words, the forgiven servant *asked* for something he was unwilling to *administer*. He asked for forgiveness. He wanted forgiveness and mercy when he was the one who had done wrong, but he wasn't willing to give forgiveness and mercy when someone else wronged him.

We are like that original servant when we fail to forgive. We want Jesus to forgive us, but we fail to show that same mercy to others. The only time we don't have to forgive is when we are sinless. "He that is without sin among you, let him first cast a stone" (John 8:7; but if we have any sin, if we've done any offense against God that He has forgiven, then we also need to forgive.

Other servants saw what happened and told the king. As you can imagine, the king was furious. He summoned the ungrateful servant and said, "You evil servant! I forgave you that tremendous debt because you pleaded with me. Shouldn't you have mercy on your fellow servant just as I had mercy on you?" (Matthew 18:32-33). The king then sent the man to prison to be tortured until he had paid his entire debt. Jesus then adds this kicker: "That's what my heavenly Father will do to you if you refuse to forgive your brothers and sisters from your heart" (v. 35).

It sounds preposterous, doesn't it? Someone is forgiven a tremendous debt, but then he turns around and squeezes a fellow debtor over a few measly dollars. This reminds me of the financial crisis in 2008 when the banks were in a panic because they had packaged phony loans and corrupted Wall Street. They begged Congress and the president to loan them trillions of dollars so the economy wouldn't collapse. Congress gave them trillions of dollars to bail them out of the crisis.

A few months later, after the banks and insurance companies got their money, do you remember what they did? They threw lavish parties and paid their executives hundreds of millions of dollars in bonuses. Then unfortunately, as far too many people know firsthand, they proceeded to throw hundreds of thousands of people out of their homes. They wouldn't let them make payments. They didn't extend any mercy. They foreclosed en masse.

Suddenly, Jesus' story isn't that hard to believe. We've lived through it in our own time. We watched it happen on our TV screens and we've read it in our newspapers. Some of us were even personally affected by it. The banks did as this wicked servant did——refused to extended forgiveness and mercy when forgiveness and mercy had been shown to them.

If you have been forgiven a great debt, what right do you have to have to make someone who owes you a small debt suffer? Likewise, if you have been forgiven for great sins, what right do you have to hold someone else's sin against them? The servant's hypocrisy in this illustration is indicative of our pettiness and unwillingness to forgive others after we have been forgiven much. Jesus says that because of the enormity of what we have been forgiven, we are obligated to forgive whatever has been done to us.

How serious is Jesus about this?

The implication Jesus makes is quite serious. If we don't forgive, we will be penalized. That's pretty clear, right?

Have you ever had someone wrong you, and you are still mad when you see that person somewhere, but they are smiling and happy? How's it make you feel?

Jesus called it "torture," and that is exactly what people describe feeling when they become filled with the pain, guilt, anger, unhappiness, stress, conflict, bitterness, and other emotional trauma that accompanies unforgiveness.

CHARACTERISTICS OF FORGIVENESS

There are five characteristics of forgiveness we can learn from this story. First, forgiveness is commanded by the Father. God freely extended forgiveness to us, so He expects forgiveness from us. That's simple and plain, but I don't say this to minimize what you've experienced in your life. I often hear people say, "But you don't know what so-and-so did!" I understand people have caused you enormous pain, but what Jesus says here is unmistakable. We have been forgiven, and we are expected to forgive.

If the pain is simply too much for you, I encourage you to please speak with a professional Christian counselor. There is no shame in having to speak to someone. I make it clear to my congregation that if they need someone to talk to, the church will help make it happen. Some pain may be too great to handle alone. For most of us, however, the issues we're holding onto aren't really as big as they seem once we step back and look at them. Certainly, in the light of all God has forgiven us, the little things that were done to us are miniscule in comparison.

Under this command to forgive, we can find guidelines for how we should forgive. Forgiveness should be given freely, with no constraints. You should not hold back forgiveness or make someone pay to get it. Don't make someone beg you to forgive him or show adequate repentance as you would perceive it before you forgive. That's not what Jesus commands. He's not saying to give the person a test and if he passes, then you can forgive him. He's saying to forgive even before they ask, even if they do not ask and even if they do not care about you forgiving him. Remember, forgiveness is for *you*.

Forgiveness should be given abundantly, not in part. "I forgive you, but I'm going to be watching you!" You're not supposed to hold your forgiveness over someone's head to control them. You can't extend forgiveness for part of what someone did and make him earn the rest. You don't want God to be stingy in His forgiveness, so don't be stingy in yours.

Forgiveness should come immediately, not over time. Remember, time doesn't heal anything. You might forget a bit of what happened in time, but that doesn't make it healed. What heals is giving forgiveness right away. When you hold on to unforgiveness for any amount of time, you jeopardize your walk with the Lord. Why risk that? Practice forgiveness regularly so that you become better at it.

If someone cuts you off in traffic, does it make sense to slam on your horn for five seconds and then forgive him or her? No, it's too late; you've already retaliated. Forgive him. Maybe he didn't see you. Maybe he's rushing to see a loved one in the hospital. What-ever the reason, it doesn't matter. You don't forgive because of him; you forgive because of who you are, a child of God.

Forgiveness should be final, without being revisited, and repeat-ed as necessary. When you forgive, you should mean it. Sometimes we have this tendency to bring stuff up after the fact. We've already said the person was forgiven. Then something reminds us of what happened and we bring it up again. There is a need to guard your mind and your mouth when you have forgiven someone. If you have truly forgiven, you shouldn't be reminding the person of the offense. Forgive and forget.

Second, forgiveness is the character of the Father. When we model forgiveness in our lives, we demonstrate God's own nature. When we forgive, we shine as an example of our heavenly Father. Choosing to forgive is a testimony of our love for Him and our willingness to obey and be His representatives. We forgive because He forgives, and we strive to be like Him. When we represent God in this way, we shine as a light to the world and draw all men to Him.

A friend of mine shared the story of when he was engaged, he had promised to give his fiancé's sixteen-year-old brother a ride to the store after he finished visiting with his fiancé at their apartment. The brother was waiting in my friend's car and had the keys be-cause he wanted to listen to the radio. Suddenly, the brother ap-peared in the apartment with his head hung low. Behind the broth-er stood an older man. All the brother said was, "I'm sorry, man."

It turned out that the brother had started my friend's car, driven it out into the street, and gotten into an accident with the man.

Instead of getting mad at the brother, my friend asked the brother if he was okay. He then asked the older man if he was okay. Both parties were fine. The boy started to cry; he wasn't working and couldn't afford to fix the car. He was embarrassed. But my friend assured him he'd take care of it and not to worry. The brother was so surprised. He'd never seen anyone react like that. He knew he was about to get beat up. But instead, he found himself forgiven. The brother started to cry even more, and my friend asked him what was wrong—was he sure he was okay? The brother said, "I ain't never met anybody like you. I want to be like you. I want to know Jesus."

When you forgive, you make Christ real for people. You become a conduit for God's love. The brother had been watching my friend. Studying him. He didn't know Christ, but he knew there was something different about my friend—different from other guys he knew. My friend had shared Christ with him in the past, but no amount of sharing could witness to this young man like the example my friend gave him when the boy wrecked the car and received forgiveness instead of a beat down. Actions truly speak louder than words.

Third, forgiveness is free, but there still may be consequences from the offenses that led us to have to forgive someone. This is because there are consequences in the natural world. However, the ultimate price of forgiveness has already been paid. Thus, we cannot demand payment of any kind from those to whom we extend forgiveness, because Jesus paid this price with His death. Forgiveness costs us nothing to receive it or to give it. To forgive the world of sin cost God the ultimate cost, His Son. Can you see why God has such a problem with us when we try to charge others for the wrongs they do to us after His Son's blood paid for our forgiveness?

Remember the servant was forgiven $25 million dollars, then tried to hurt someone over a few thousand dollars. This is how

God sees the price Jesus paid for our sins verses the price we want others to pay when they hurt us. When we forgive people, we recognize the great price that our own sins cost God. In light of that price, we cannot demand payment from others.

Fourth, forgiveness is a choice of faith, not an emotion. When we don't understand forgiveness, we sometimes believe we should forgive only when we feel like forgiving. There is an old saying about emotions: "Emotions make a great servant but a poor master." When we forgive, we make a conscious choice of faith. If we wait until we feel like forgiving, we may never get around to it. It's not about how we feel; it's about being obedient to God's Word.

Finally, forgiveness is critical to our freedom. In Africa, monkeys are captured in an interesting way. Trappers use small cages with bait inside. The monkeys are smart enough not to enter the cage, so they reach through the bars. There's only one problem: The bait inside the cage is larger than the space between the bars. The only way for the monkeys to remove their hands is to let go of the bait, but the monkeys refuse to let go of the bait.

If we refuse to let go of unforgiveness, we are like those trapped monkeys. Except Satan is the one who traps us. We must let go of unforgiveness to find freedom. It's not about what the other person deserves or whether they apologize; it is about our own freedom. If we stay in anger, we only grow more angry. If we forgive, we experience forgiveness ourselves. Our unwillingness to forgive and liberate others traps us. If we can understand unforgiveness in this way, we will quickly see how pointless it is to hold onto hurts. Let them go for your own sake, regardless of whether you ever get reconciliation with the person who hurt you. Regardless of whether an apology ever comes. Just let it go.

BURY YOUR BAG

This ugly utility bag of unforgiveness is such a horrible thing to carry around that simply tossing it is not always the best way to make sure you don't go back and pick it up again. When it comes to this particular piece of emotional baggage, I like to hold an actual funeral service for it and bury it. Literally. I'm going to suggest you do that with any unforgiveness you hold in your heart.

Here's how this works. Take a sheet of paper and write "I Choose to Forgive . . ." Then list everyone and everything you have failed to forgive in your life—the people who have hurt you, the things that have happened to you, even the things you hold against yourself. Then write "I Choose to Forgive Them for . . ." and include the events, the crimes, the wrongs, the humiliations, the mistakes, the sins others have done to you. If the person you need to forgive is yourself, write "I Choose to Forgive Myself for . . ." and include what you did, who you did it to, and when you did it. Be as detailed as necessary to touch on each feeling of pain, guilt, anger, and vengeance you have.

The purpose of this funeral is to help you renew your mind. True forgiveness will not occur unless you have a renewing of your mind. You must learn to think differently about the things that have happened. The funeral is to help you bury these things so that you understand, once and for all, that they are gone, past, over, and done, and you can now get on with your life.

Once you have written the name of each person you want to forgive and the thing for which you are forgiving them, take that piece of paper, ball it up, and bury it. If you have a yard, bury it there. Not in a garden, though. I don't want you accidentally digging it up again in the spring. If you don't have a yard, cremate it in the fireplace, in the barbeque grill, or carefully over your kitchen sink. If you're uncomfortable with fire, bury it in the trash and throw the trash out. You can even have a little ceremony or a last farewell when the garbage truck comes by and hauls it away.

But here's the key: Once you get rid of that paper, everything on it is dead to you. The issues are gone. They are forgiven. Mark the date on your calendar as the day those issues died. Never allow that thing, that person, that crime, that insult, that injury to ever burden your mind again. If for some reason, you're reminded of them, repeat to yourself that they are dead.

Sometimes we will forget that something or someone has been buried. Someone could have passed away, but one day you wake up and think about that person and pick up the phone to call him. But what happens when you remember? You put the phone down. That's how those issues should be if they ever come up again. You see the person who wronged you, and you don't review, rehearse, or react to what happened. It's gone. You have forgiven.

This may not be easy at first, but it will get easier with practice. And it may be easier than you think. Still, there are six proofs that help us know we have truly extended forgiveness to others.

PROOFS OF FORGIVENESS

The first proof is that we are able to articulate what we learned from the experience. Ask yourself, "What has God taught me through this experience?" When you can answer this question without bitterness and understand that there was something beneficial you gained from the experience, it is a sign you have truly forgiven the person or event. Remember, God said all things work together for our good. If we can see the good from it or if we have learned a valuable lesson and can appreciate that lesson, then we know we have forgiven.

The second proof is when we can talk about the experience without being gripped by feelings of resentment and revenge. One of the techniques of a therapist is to have a victim or client who has experienced trauma retell his or her story multiple times. Each time the client does this, the therapist helps him or her desensitize from the trauma and reframe the negative cognitions related to the event so that the memory does not continue to victimize the client but helps the client instead see that he or she has survived— overcome, beaten it, won. When we are able to talk about what happened without feeling the pain of guilt, shame, resentment, and revenge, then we have truly grown, learned, and forgiven.

The third proof is when we are able to recognize that perhaps we may have played a part in creating the hurt that impacted us. This does not mean that we caused the event, but that we may have extended the hurt through unforgiveness. It's called recognizing our part. Similar to the second proof listed above, when we gain some distance from things, we usually are able to stop seeing ourselves only as victims of what happened. When we can begin to understand that part of the pain we suffered came from our refusal to forgive what happened to us, we have evidence that we have forgiven.

The fourth proof is when we can revisit the scene, either physically or in our imaginations, without experiencing debilitating negative reactions. Again, this is related to being free from the victimization. When you can remember what happened without becoming angry, hurt, or negative again, you have good evidence of having forgiven.

The fifth proof is when we are able to actively pursue the benefit and welfare of those who have wronged us. This isn't always possible, but if we can, it is great evidence that we have forgiven. When you can pray, "Lord, bless this person," then you know you've been healed. This is the place God wants you. If you can't pray for the person who hurt you, then you likely still have some unforgiveness in your heart, which is where Satan wants you. God wants you free. Satan wants you trapped like that monkey at that cage. If it's a struggle, keep forgiving; eventually, you will get past it.

The sixth proof is when we no longer need to rehearse the details of the experience or event that caused us pain with others. This means we no longer talk about it. We don't bring it up to friends and family. We don't write blogs about it. We don't tweet about it or post on Facebook about it. We don't remind people about it. We are done with it. It is dead and buried and behind us. When we reach this point, we have good evidence that we have forgiven.

The ugly utility bag of unforgiveness is the bulkiest, heaviest, most awkward, and cumbersome emotional bag we can carry. There are no handles on it. It flops all over our shoulders, our heads, our arms, and backs. It's unwieldy, top-heavy, and drags on the floor behind us, leaking its contents for anyone who follows us to trip over. The longer we carry it, the more we hurt ourselves, our relationships, and our fellowship with God. It's full of toxic waste that threatens our health, spirit, and sanity. Unloading it will lighten our load tremendously, but it is best to bury it or burn it because we can't afford to run the risk of picking this bag up ever again.

[1]*Conformed to His Image: Biblical and Practical Approaches to Spiritual Formation*, by Dr. Kenneth Boa (Zondervan, 2001).

[2]*The Speaker's Quote Book*, by Roy B. Zuck (Kregal, 2009); page 198.

[3]"Number of American Adults Who Can't Read," at http://www.statisticbrain.com/number-of-american-adults-who-cant-read/.

[4]*The Speaker's Quote Book*; page 555.

[5]"See It Through," by Edgar A. Guest, Public Domain.

[6]*Too Soon to Quit!: Fifteen Achievers From the Bible Teach Us How to Keep Going and How to Finish Well*, by Warren W. Wiersbe (CLC Publications, 2001); page 40.

by Warren W. Wiersbe

[7]Mark Tyrrell

[8]*Confessions*, by Augustine of Hippo, translated by William Watts (Harvard University Press, 1912); page 1.

[9]"The Wardrobe of Easter: Forgiveness" at http://worship.calvin.edu/resources/resource-library/the-wardrobe-of-easter-forgiveness.

[10]*Love Must Be Tough: New Hope for Marriages in Crisis*, by Dr. James C. Dobson (Tyndale, 2007).

[11]Dr. Steven R. Covey at https://www.stephencovey.com.

CONCLUSION

"Wherefore seeing we also are compassed about with so great a cloud of witnesses, let us lay aside every weight, and the sin which doth so easily beset us, and let us run with patience the race that is set before us."
(Hebrews 12:1)

A recent survey published on TheMail.com says that the majority of us over-pack by two thirds. That means many of us only need one third of the stuff we pack in our luggage on a typical trip. Turns out I'm not alone in my struggle to get my wife to travel lightly. According to the survey, women pack the most. They even use their husband's bags to pack, and it is one of the most common arguments between couples on trips.

Can you imagine what it might be like to carry sixty-six percent less luggage on your next trip? What a relief! No more struggling with bags that refuse to zip. No more lugging that heavy weight down the stairs and into the car. No more standing in the long lines to check your bags. No more searching to locate the baggage claim. No more losing your luggage. No more waiting for your stuff to come around on the carousel.

I'm a living testimony that the benefits are endless. I hope you will try it for yourself on your next trip.

I'm still working on Cleo.

If you decide you would rather keep your heavy suitcases when you travel the world, at least take God up on His offer to help you unload your emotional baggage. Although Cleo hasn't chosen to travel lightly through airports yet, she fully embraces the concept of traveling lightly when it comes to emotional baggage. We may over-pack by sixty-six percent when we travel on planes, trains, and automobiles, but I'm going to argue that we do far worse when it comes to emotional baggage.

I believe ninety percent of the emotional stuff you deal with every single day of your life is stuff you absolutely do not need in your mind, body, or spirit. That means only one of the ten emotional bags you carry belongs in your life. You should dump nine of those bags on the ground and leave them permanently behind.

What about that tenth bag?

That's the one you should give to God.

You may be thinking, *Where do you get that number?*

Author Steven Covey came up with a wonderful principle he calls the "90–10 Rule." It's simple and makes a lot of sense: "Ten percent of life is made up of what happens to you. Ninety percent of life is decided by how you react."[11]

We have no control over 10 percent of what happens to us. For instance, you can't stop the train from being late or make the weather better. You can't change whether you were born rich or poor. You can't alter the things that happened to you in the past. There are parts of life you have absolutely no control over, but those parts amount to only ten percent.

However, the other 90 percent is different. You determine that by your reaction to the ten percent.

Let me give you an example. During breakfast with your family, your son reaches across the table and accidentally knocks a glass of milk onto your suit. You've told him a hundred times not to reach across the table. Still, you have no control over what happened. However, what happens next depends on your reaction.

You get mad, jump up, and holler at your son, reminding him how careless he is and how he ignored all the times you told him this would happen if he kept reaching across the table. You make him feel horrible, and he gets upset. Then you turn to your wife and tell her she put too much milk in the glass or put it too close to the edge of the table or shouldn't have served milk. Now she's mad as well, and you two are arguing.

You yell on the way to change your suit. Your son is so upset that he neglected to get ready for school, so he misses the bus. Now you have to drive him. On the way, you realize you're running late. The light turned yellow two seconds ago, but you figure you've got time. The cop doesn't see it that way, and now you have a $480 ticket for running a red light. You drop your son off with no high-five, no hug, and no "Have a good day, buddy" like you usually do.

You're thirty minutes late to work, and when you get there you realize you forgot the report you had to turn in. It's at home along with your briefcase and cell phone. You finally get home that night, looking forward to dinner and relaxing. Instead, your wife is ticked off, your son isn't talking to you, and there's nothing to eat for dinner.

Why? All of this happened because of the way you reacted to the spilled milk. Think about it. Why did you have a horrible day? Because of your son? The milk? The cop who gave you a ticket? The answer is because of *you*. Because of your reaction. It was all on you. You couldn't control the spilled milk, but you could have reacted differently to it.

Imagine if, instead, you had calmly looked at your son and said, "Hey, remember we talked about this. You have to be careful."

He would have said, "Oops, I'm sorry, Daddy. I'll be more careful next time."

You could have changed your suit, come back down in time to give him a hug and see him to the bus, grab your report, briefcase, and cell phone, and leave for work. You could have arrived to work on time an—guess what? You would have had a great day. Big, big difference, right? All because of the way you chose to react over spilled milk. Getting rid of emotional baggage is basically about applying this principle to your life on a daily basis.

Imagine a simple run to the grocery. You are in a pleasant mood and say good morning to the cashier at the checkout. He ignores you. After he rings you up, he drops your change on the counter, and turns to greet the next customer. Guess what? That's not your problem. Emotional baggage can make it your problem, but it's really not your problem. Whatever is going on in his life was there before you arrived at the store, and it will be there after you leave.

You don't have to react to it. You can, but you don't have to. You could open up the attaché case of anxiety and imagine all the reasons he treated you that way. You could explore the depths of the luggage of low self-esteem and recall all the other people in your life who didn't give you due respect. You could rummage through your backpack of bitterness and ask to see his boss and return all the groceries. You could even grab an option from the utility bag of unforgiveness and try to get him fired.

You could, but you don't have to. You don't need to pack that experience in your duffle bag of depression, doubt, and defeatism. You don't have to absorb his negativity in your life. You don't have to have a bad day because the checkout boy had a less than pleasant attitude.

Instead, you could give him grace like Christ gives you. After all, maybe he just lost a loved one. Maybe he got some other bad news. Maybe he didn't realize how he reacted to you. Maybe he didn't ignore you at all and did say good morning, but you missed it. It doesn't matter. What matters is whether you carry emotional baggage out of that store along with your groceries.

Getting rid of your emotional baggage will keep you from reacting negatively to the 10 percent of life you cannot control. Truly, you have no need to be burdened with depression, doubt, defeatism, anxiety, hopelessness, discouragement, guilt, people-pleasing, low self-esteem, fear, bitterness, and unforgiveness. All of these bags are too heavy to carry.

We began this book with Hebrews 12:1, and I want us to end it with this Scripture as well: "Wherefore seeing we also are compassed about with so great a cloud of witnesses, let us lay aside every weight, and the sin which doth so easily beset us, and let us run with patience the race that is set before us."

As I conclude this book and thank you for joining me on this journey, let me point out one final thing about that Scripture: It is only after you lay aside these heavy weights and excess baggage that you begin to run your race.

Wondering what were you doing before? You were lugging

around a bunch of excess baggage you didn't need. You were unable to run because you were burdened down. Once you're free of the excess baggage, you can run the race God has destined for you.

Be patient with yourself during this process. Notice the race is to be run "with patience, namely endurance and perseverance." Change happens the instant you make a decision to change, but old habits can sometimes seem hard to break. Be optimistic and determined as you apply the principles we've discussed. Remember, sometimes the one most in need of your forgiveness is *you*.

Until next time, *Travel Lightly*.

ABOUT THE AUTHOR

Dr. Craig L. Oliver, Sr. is the senior pastor of Elizabeth Baptist Church. His passionate yet pedagogic approach to preaching touches hearts, fortifies spirits, and transforms the minds of believers and nonbelievers across the world. With a faith rooted and grounded in the Word of God, Pastor Oliver desires to fulfill the Great Commission by sharing the R.E.A.L. Experience—**R**estoring Hope, **E**mpowering People, **A**dvancing the Kingdom, and **L**eaving a Legacy.

Dr. Oliver's twenty-four years of ministry have been anointed by God and personify Ephesians 3:20: "Now unto him that is able to do exceeding abundantly above all that we ask or think, according to the power that worketh in us."

Since receiving and accepting his calling at the young age of sixteen and becoming pastor of Elizabeth Baptist Church at the age of twenty-one, Dr. Craig L. Oliver, Sr. has seen the hand of God expand Elizabeth Baptist Church by over 16,000 members and to five locations within the Metro Atlanta area. Under his leadership, the church has completed mission work within the local Atlanta community and abroad in over six countries, with more on the horizon. His style of preaching connects with those desperate for the unadulterated truth of God's Word through twelve weekly services, weekly television broadcasts, and via the Internet at www.freshmannatv.com.

Dr. Oliver holds multiple degrees, including a master of arts in biblical/theological studies and leadership from Luther Rice Theological Seminary and a doctoral degree from Gordon Conwell Theological Seminary. Though this dynamic man of God has received a myriad of accolades, Pastor Oliver carefully marries the tradition of sound preaching with the understanding that as Jesus met those in need where they were, so should we. He delivers practical points, knowing that the best sermon ever heard is the last one that is actually put into practice.

At the heart of this great man of God is his love for his family. Pastor Oliver's joy and balance is his wife, First Lady Chi'Ira, and three beautiful children: son, Craig Jr., and daughters, Corrie, Kené, and Charlee Reign. As a dynamic ministry family, they are dedicated servants of God and stand as a testament to what God can do in the lives of true believers!